REMARKABLE

Stories from mamapreneurs who have
created success despite the odds

REMARKABLE

Stories from mamapreneurs who have
created success despite the odds

LIANNE KIM

ALI MILLER | LILY HORBATIUK | FRANCES MURRAY
LAURA ENGEN | AMANDA CASINHA | NANCY MACDONALD
MELANIE ZILTENER | ADRIENNE SHNIER | CHERNELL BARTHOLOMEW
LEA PICKARD | LUSIANA LUKMAN | MEAGHAN BEAMES
SAMANTHA VLASCEANU | CHERYL MASON

TABLE OF CONTENTS

THE COURAGE TO LEAP   8
Lianne Kim

MAKING THE MOM LIFE OF YOUR DREAMS
A REALITY!   20
Dr. Ali Miller

FINDING PURPOSE THROUGH MOTHERHOOD   35
Lily Horbatiuk

NO, I GET TO CHOOSE   46
Frances Murray

CHASING MOTHERHOOD DREAMS AND
BUSINESS SUCCESS   59
Laura Engen

GROWING THROUGH GRIEF   72
Amanda Casinha

THE BLANK CANVAS   86
Nancy Macdonald

WHY NOT ME?   99
Melanie Ziltener

APPLY YOURSELF: ADVANCING FROM
SCARCITY TO ABUNDANCE   111
Adrienne Shnier

SEEN BUT NOT HEARD   128
Chernell Bartholomew

REMEMBER YOUR WILD   141
Lea Pickard

THE LOTUS FLOWER   157
Lusiana Lukman

BEING BRAVE IS ASKING FOR HELP   171
Meaghan Beames

FAIL NOW TO SUCCEED TOMORROW   185
Samantha Vlasceanu

AT THE COST OF EVERYTHING   197
Cheryl Mason

CONCLUSION   210
Lianne Kim

LIANNE KIM

Lianne Kim is a business coach and the founder of Mamas & Co.—
a community for mama entrepreneurs. She is the host of the wildly
popular podcast *The Business of Thinking Big* and the author of the
best-selling book *Building a Joyful Business*. Lianne is on a mission
to help women make a great living on their own terms, doing what
they love.

WHAT WOULD IT LOOK LIKE IF I DIDN'T NEED A JOB? WHAT IF I COULD BE MY OWN BOSS DOING SOMETHING I LOVE?

LIANNE KIM

THE COURAGE TO LEAP

What would it look like if I didn't need a job? What if I could be my own boss doing something I love?

—Lianne Kim

I was in my late thirties when I asked myself these questions. It was a Monday morning, and I had just walked out of my boss's office. According to her, my performance was slipping, and I was not giving the 110 percent they had come to expect from me. I was not the "team player" they required, so I had to step it up, or else. I sauntered out of that office, slack-jawed and dumbfounded. I had given that company six years of my life. I had some of the best sales on the team. I consistently helped train and mentor the newer hires, willingly sharing my systems and processes I'd developed over the years so that they, too, could be great salespeople.

But it wasn't enough.

Had my performance slipped? Probably.

You see, since starting at that company, I'd had two kids in two years. I now had to juggle a full-time career and motherhood, and I was not managing things well. I liked my job well enough, but I felt tethered to something that didn't give me much personal fulfillment. I wanted to be available for my children, but I needed to make a living and support the family, which meant I didn't have as much time with them as I would have liked. I was being pulled in a million directions, and I felt drained. I felt like I was giving all I could in every aspect of my life, but it felt like I was trying to "pour from an empty cup," as the expression goes.

And now this? My employer questioning my performance?

As I rode the subway home, I recall feeling a sense of deep shame. I started recounting all the ways this job was not feeling aligned for me. I had always been a good soldier, but this incident made me feel dejected and unvalued. I had ideas for how we could improve things on the team, but nobody in management seemed interested. I was meant to bring in as many sales as I could, but there seemed no way for me to contribute on a more meaningful level. I was good at my job, but the passion had faded. Most importantly, I felt like I was busting my ass to make someone else millions of dollars, but I was seeing very little of that.

As I sat on that bustling, crowded subway, my head in my hands, I started calculating my options.

Option A: Stay at this job and feel unappreciated and undervalued. The thought of this option made my stomach turn.

Option B: Quit and be a stay-at-home mom. Again, this was not really an option, as my family needed the income.

Option C: Find a new job. This idea felt overwhelming to me, as I already felt stretched thin and knew that a job hunt, applications, and interviewing all took an immense amount of mental and emotional energy.

Option D: Find a way to make a living for myself, without needing a job. This last option felt intriguing and exciting but also very scary. After all, I didn't know the first thing about being self-employed. This idea made me feel nervous and anxious . . . and yet I couldn't stop wondering . . .

Could I really do it? Could I be my own boss?

Now, becoming self-employed might sound simple enough, but you have to understand that I felt in over my head. My days were filled with picking up and dropping off at daycare, raising two babies, making dinner, and keeping our home running smoothly, not to mention all the duties my nine-to-five job required of me. I felt overwhelmed almost every minute of every day. I didn't have a moment to breathe let alone begin planning my entrepreneurial endeavors.

I had no idea where I would get the time or energy to launch a business.

I was also struggling with a deep sense of unworthiness, partly because I felt like I was failing at my job (*how could I run a business if I wasn't even succeeding at a day job?*) but also because I felt like I was failing at life. I barely saw my kids, there was never enough time for anything, I was always in a rush, my marriage was struggling, I hardly ever saw my friends . . .

Along with this sense of "failing at life," I had a very troubling sense of impostor syndrome. I lay awake at night, wondering who would ever choose me as a sales consultant (my original business idea). I didn't have the same clout or experience as all the other people I had seen in this type of role over my years in sales. I had never consulted before. I had no idea how to package or price my services. I had no real prospects. I was plagued by self-sabotaging thoughts of "I'm not good enough." (I later learned this feeling is very common in entrepreneurship, but at the time, I was quite new to navigating these very big feelings.)

So there I was, unhappy with my job, wanting to quit to pursue my dreams of being my own boss and calling the shots, but I felt immobilized with fear and self-doubt.

But one thing in my life made all the difference . . . **my community**.

By this time, I had been running *Mamas & Co.* for a few years as a hobby. I had cultivated a wonderful group of women—all moms—who were also starting their own businesses. We would meet up on a monthly basis to talk about our lives and share our knowledge with one another. In these women, I had regular examples of people who had done what I wanted to do—overcome the odds to earn a living on their own terms.

Together, the community members and I started setting goals, supporting one another, and holding each other accountable. We started connecting online and off-line so we could keep the momentum going. These women had my back, and I, in turn, had theirs. If one of us didn't have the answer to something, someone in the group would step in to lend a hand. I also chose to hire a business coach, and wow! What a difference that made. Having a mentor who believed in me, who could pass along the knowledge she had gleaned through the years, truly helped me fast-track my dreams.

After many months of contemplating, I made the leap to self employment in late 2016. And while I thought I was going to be a "Sales Consultant," my role quickly shifted to that of "Business Coach." I was connecting with female entrepreneurs regularly and learning all about their problems, and guess what? Their problems were the exact type of situations with which I was able to help. I was teaching these women about sales, as well as a lot of things related to running and growing a business. I coached them on marketing, social media, public speaking, business finances, operations, and most importantly, the mindset needed to achieve success in business.

Soon, these women were calling me their "coach," and I liked the sound of that. It made me feel like the trusted helper I longed to be. It gave me a sense of purpose I had been lacking in my old sales job. Client by client, hour by hour, I started to actually feel like the leader they saw me as: someone with almost two decades of experience in sales and marketing; someone with a ton of experience in teaching and leadership.

I was no longer *trying* to be a business coach, I was one.

My first true Dream Client—the kind that you have to pinch yourself because they are so perfect—was a woman named Sara. Sara had a successful blog and website and had made quite a name for herself in the green living space. She had recently pivoted her business to social media management. She had several paying clients and recurring monthly revenue. She was kind, smart, and hardworking, and she had developed a strong network of clients and peers during her journey. She was building her empire, but along the way, she had hit a few road bumps. She knew working with a coach would help her reach her goals further and faster, so she approached me.

At that time, I remember thinking, *really? She wants ME to be her coach? She seems so experienced, so accomplished! Why would she want to hire me?*

And then I remembered something that my first coach said to me: "You don't have to be a million miles ahead of someone to coach them, you just need to be that little bit further."

I did coach Sara and many other women, and as time went by, I began to realize two things:

1. I am *really* good at this!
and
2. These women are truly incredible.

And it was true. I was good at my job. I had honed my craft, developed my coaching skills, and invented several systems and frameworks that were getting a lot of women BIG results. I had developed a strong online presence. I was getting asked to speak at events. I was receiving inquiries and referrals regularly. Where I once feared I wouldn't have enough business, I now realized that there were more than enough people who needed my support and were willing to pay for it.

It was also true that the women I was attracting to my community and my programs were genuinely outstanding. They were setting goals and taking action. They were moving forward, despite the bumps in the road, and not only that, they were also helping the women around them do the same thing. They were courageous and determined.

They were, in a word . . . REMARKABLE.

Remarkable is not a word I use lightly, by the way. Don't believe me? Here are a few of the accomplishments the women I coach have achieved:

- Going back to school as a mature student to learn a new craft.
- Overcoming abuse to build outstanding businesses.
- Combating racism, sexism, and countless other forms of bias through their work.
- Surviving physical and mental trauma and helping others do the same.
- Paving the way for the next generation of female entrepreneurs through their mentorship and support.
- Giving others a leg up in their journey through their philanthropic endeavors.

As the years went on, I couldn't help but notice how the women I was coaching were not only changing their own lives but also the lives of so many others in the process.

In fact, my women employ a lot of other women. My women lift others up with their content, books, courses, and podcasts. My women question societal norms and create movements for positive change. My women do it all with grace and tenacity (and a side dose of *badassery*), all while raising children, running a household, being a supportive partner, daughter, friend.

My women are quite literally **changing the world**.

So, when I call them "remarkable," please know that it is no embellishment. I mean it with every fiber of my being.

A few years ago, I had the good fortune of coaching a woman named Sabrina Greer who had founded a company called *YGTMedia*, and through our work together I learned a) what a badass she was (naturally!), and b) all about book publishing. Because of our work together, I got the bug to write all my greatest lessons about entrepreneurship in my first book, *Building a Joyful Business*, and you know what? I loved it so much I just had to do it again.

Joyful Business was meant to be my legacy. It was all my greatest lessons about running a business . . . joyfully. It was about the hard lessons I learned that I didn't want anyone to have to go through. It was the blueprint for having both the life and the business of your dreams. I wanted people to feel like they could have the support of a successful, seasoned business coach without breaking the bank. I wanted every woman who had a desire of being her own boss to get the fast-track to success, joy, and freedom. I wanted to share all my trade secrets in one short, powerful book so that anyone who wanted to do what I had done could do so, all for under $25!

With *Remarkable*, I wanted to take that mission one step further. This book wasn't going to be another "how-to" business guide but rather an inspirational message of hope that spans every industry, race, age and stage, and business type.

When I first spoke with Sabrina about this project, I said, "This book is for that new 'mamapreneur' who has a dream of becoming a business owner but is scared to make the leap. It's examples of moms who have overcome the odds to build remarkable businesses and lives for themselves, not only despite the setbacks but, as you'll see, often because of them. It's the book I needed when I was first starting out."

And so, dear reader, I share with you fourteen powerful stories of grit, perseverance, heartache, success, failure, and all the little twists and turns in between. I share with you women, mothers, who have not only made a great living on their own terms doing what they love but who have also done so courageously, through pain, hardship, and trauma.

These women are truly remarkable, and I consider myself honored to know them. We all need mentors who have gone before, who have lived the hard lessons and come through the other side, so we may know that it is possible for us to do the same.

WE ALL NEED EXAMPLES OF WHAT IS POSSIBLE.

Adrienne, Ali, Amanda, Chernell, Cheryl, Fran, Laura, Lea, Lily, Lusiana, Meaghan, Melanie, Nancy, and Samantha: Thank you for saying yes to this project and making it a priority in your busy lives. Thank you for being incredibly open and coachable through this process, as

I know firsthand that publishing a book is not for the faint of heart. Thank you for always keeping the needs of our readers top of mind as you divulge your wisdom and lessons. Thank you for being brave and vulnerable and for your willingness to share from your scars in the hopes that it might help others heal as well.

Reader, as you thumb through these stories, may they act as a reminder that we all have infinite wisdom and potential inside of us, and that anything you wish to achieve in your life and business is absolutely within reach.

Enjoy!

IT WASN'T UP TO EVERYONE ELSE TO DECIDE WHAT I DO. I AM CREATING MY LIFE AND WHAT WORKS FOR ME.

DR. ALI MILLER

DR. ALI MILLER

Master scheduler and organizer for a family of five but cannot remember the lyrics to any song. Disciplined enough to exercise daily but will crush a line of Oreos at any opportunity. Competitive cheerleader for others but hates to lose at ANY game. Pediatric chiropractor by day and always a true "kid" at heart. A Leo who loves her parents dearly, adores her friends, and appreciates that there is no better time than a kitchen dance party with her family of five.

Website: www.familyhealthchiropractic.ca

FB/IG: @dralimiller

To my parents, for teaching me love and for giving me the opportunity to go after my dreams. To my husband, Adam, for making me the mother of three beautiful and strong women. Thank you for unleashing my confidence, for supporting me in every way possible, and for always bringing the fun in life. To my girls, Riley, Bailey, and Zoe: You have taught me so much more than I could have ever imagined. Thank you for being the very definition of strength and vulnerability.

CHAPTER 1

MAKING THE MOM LIFE OF YOUR DREAMS A REALITY!

I remember being a little girl and looking forward to being a mama one day. I had a plenitude of dolls to prove it. They had multiple outfits that I would change them into depending on what activity we were doing. I took them to dinner, to church, on vacation, and to my brother's hockey games. They were my babies. I played school with them. I pretended to take them to activities. They had their places to sleep, and I made sure to cover them with a blanket at bedtime. I wanted them to feel safe. I envisioned the day when I would have real babies to take care of, raise, and keep safe.

I had no idea motherhood was so much more than diapers and activities. I was unaware of everything I wanted to share with my girls as they grew up: how I wanted them to be fearless in trying new things; how I wanted them to be brave and know they could do anything. I wanted them to be strong and confident, and in my most recent learning, I wanted them to know that being vulnerable and asking for help does not mean you are weak. In fact, it is the opposite. *There is strength in vulnerability.*

I met my future husband when I was only nineteen. A youngin'. He was older than me and already entering his professional career. I knew fairly quickly I wanted this man to be the father of my children. I continued with my university degree while he started work. I was already thinking of the next step of marriage and family, but he was quick to let me know it wasn't time yet. Shortly after I graduated, on a surprise weekend away, he popped the question. Without a doubt in my mind, I said yes, and we began the planning. I took a year after graduating to work and save money as we planned the wedding. It was at this time that I applied and was accepted to what would become my future career as a chiropractor. Everything was seamlessly fitting into place. Partner, check. Down payment on our first condo, check. Career, check.

STARTING SCHOOL

Chiropractic school is far from easy. It is a four-year program that sometimes has you taking twelve courses at the same time. Classes run between September and May, with summer off for years one and two. The third year continues right through the summer to finish off the fourth year just in time for graduation in the spring of the final year. We decided that trying to have our baby between the second and third years would be ideal. I would take the next year off and join the class one year behind for the third year.

We had zero issues conceiving when we wanted, and the expected due date was the end of July. Aside from being nervous about telling my parents that I had actually participated in sex to make this baby, things were great. That is until I went to speak with the dean of our school to fill him in on our plan of taking the year off and my coming back twelve months later. It was a hard no. The school had changed the curriculum: my class was in the final year of the old curriculum, meaning there was no option to take a year off. I would need to continue my studies with a baby in tow. The next two years were going to be far from easy, but I was assured the school would help me where they could. I don't think I completely understood how I would need to lean on others in the coming years.

Chiropractic school taught me many core lessons about where health comes from and how our body heals. In studying pregnancy and pediatrics, I gained confidence in how strong and smart a woman's body is, and I was prepared to have my baby naturally. The day I went into labor is the day that my life changed forever. I learned the true strength of being a woman. I learned the innate ability of our body to know when it is time to birth a baby. Although much of life to date seemed to go along with the plan, the afternoon I went into labor did not. My body let me know what was happening. We had chosen midwives to deliver our baby, and my husband was in communication with them as I started labor. I don't remember feeling nervous. I knew I could handle what came my way.

When the midwives arrived at our condo, they let us know things had progressed so quickly that we would not make it to the hospital. I was in no place to debate or argue, and to my surprise, a short time later we were a family of three cuddling in our bed. It was beautiful. We never made it to the hospital in the end! Outside of a LOT of extra laundry and stressing our family members, everything had gone perfectly.

I have always respected and been amazed by anyone who accomplishes a big physical task: a hockey team winning the Stanley Cup, an Ironman athlete crossing the finish line, or a beautiful ballerina on broken point shoes. Childbirth is by far the most incredible example of strength there is. During this exhibition of strength, women surrender to their bodies and have their hearts explode in gaining the title of Mom. Women are champions.

LEANING ON MY VILLAGE

Five weeks after giving birth, I entered my third year of chiropractic school. I didn't think much of it. I didn't have all the answers about what was to come, but I took it one day at a time. I leaned on the village. There were parts of my day at school that were hands-on, and I had wonderful classmates with opposite schedules who took their turns watching the baby. I had one day a week that was extremely busy at school, and we had family members and friends who took a day off to watch our beautiful baby. I had profs who paced the front of a lecture hall holding our baby so I could write a test. My husband spent many a night playing and walking with our baby while I was studying. We co-slept because this was survival. My husband had to get up for work in the morning, and I had to function for school and for our little baby girl who really loved the warmth of sleeping with her mom and dad. This was the best way for everyone to get the necessary rest.

The next year and a half was a bit of a blur, but I know I would not have been able to do it alone. There were moments when I wondered what I was doing. Stressful moments of juggling a young child and trying to study for exams. My emotions were all over the place. I would be enjoying a cute smile with our baby one moment and then in the next moment have anxiety if she wouldn't settle while I was trying to study for a test the next day. I would get angry at others when they complained about everything they had to get done. It was during this time I learned some big lessons. **There is no place for comparison to others**. It wasn't fair to me to put the expectation on myself that my marks should and could be as high as others who were solely focused on their studies. I wasn't living the carefree life of a mid-twenty-year-old with bar nights and sleep-ins. And although there were days when that seemed pretty appealing, I was content in jumping in quickly with both feet to adulthood, marriage, and parenthood.

FACING CHALLENGES

Heading into the fourth year, we felt like we had this parenting thing mastered. We decided to continue with our family and became pregnant quite quickly. Contrary to my first pregnancy where I didn't tell anyone until five months pregnant, I was confident about telling people early in the pregnancy at around eight weeks. Just two weeks later, I went to the bathroom to discover some spotting. It was followed by some cramping. I'm not sure if I was naive or in denial, but I didn't go right into stress mode. I scheduled an ultrasound the next day, and after dropping our daughter at daycare, I went to my appointment. I didn't share what was happening with anyone other than my husband.

At this point in my life, I was still too tough to show vulnerability. I didn't ask for help or lean on friends or family when it came to supporting me. I was okay with their help when it came to my daughter, but for some reason, I felt like I had to handle things myself when it came to me. For this reason, I went to the ultrasound appointment by myself. I remember the radiologist coming to my room shortly after the tech left to let me know I had lost the baby. I was in shock. Was this my fault? How embarrassing to tell everyone after just sharing with them that I was pregnant! Does this mean I will never carry another baby? I called my husband on the way to my GP. I was sad, but I don't think I really sat in my feelings or even let myself feel them. It was almost as if I heard the news, accepted it, put on a brave face, and moved on. Where did this toughness come from? Was I actually tough, or was it all a facade?

The next six months were challenge upon challenge. We had listed our condo and bought our first home. Our daughter was in that busy toddler stage. School was winding down, and I was trying to put the time into getting ready to write three days of board exams. We decided to try to have another baby and were successful in conceiving once again. I was newly pregnant and very tired.

In the springtime, my husband got very sick. He has struggled with bowel disease since I met him, and this flare-up landed him on our couch for months. There is pain, there is weight loss, there is a lack of energy—and there's me, the "fixer." Being part of the natural health-care field, I looked up nutrition changes to help him. I wanted him to see a chiropractor and be adjusted. I was trying to be supportive and improve his mood. It was hard to not have him feeling well enough to help me out, and it was sad to not be able to do things as a family. I would get mad at myself for thinking these thoughts, as it wasn't his fault that he wasn't well. I was still wrapping up school and keeping a toddler busy. On the outside, I looked like I was handling all of it with grace. On the inside, it was a lot.

I crossed the stage to receive my degree as my husband's health improved. I wrote the last part of my practical board exams and breathed a sigh of relief as this chapter closed. I could enjoy being a mom for two months before baby arrived.

Knowing that preparation is key and that my labor and deliveries seemed to move quite quickly, we were ready and planned for a home birth this time. Our second daughter, or "baby sista" as our eldest referred to her during my pregnancy, was born two weeks early in the home we still live in. This delivery, of course, had its own excitement and story. I remember my husband frantically pulling out shoelaces in case the midwives didn't make it and he had to deliver the baby on his own. Our two-year-old slept through it all, and that night, we became a family of four.

I was in no rush to get into practice. I was happy to take a breather and get accustomed to this new mom life once again. I did library programs, mom-and-tot swims, and playdates. I loved it. This is the image I dreamed of when I had my dolls. I was made for this.

The next winter, our two-and-a-half-year-old had a tobogganing accident and broke her leg. Small setback to an independent toddler and to her mom who was carrying around a seven-month-old. I would have never imagined that a life lesson would present itself to me at the check-out of a grocery store. I had our toddler sitting in the bottom of the cart with her leg outstretched in a cast. The baby infant seat was placed in the top section of the cart. As the cashier rang through my groceries, I loaded the bags into all the open spaces. A separate employee from the store came over and said she could help me out to the car. I said, "No worries, I've got it."

She looked me in the eye and said, "I know you're okay, but it's also okay for someone to help you."

At the time, I didn't realize how impactful that statement was. It's not like I don't like help, and it's not like I don't like helping others. Why was there this resistance to being vulnerable or accepting the help when it came to me? It has taken many years for me to be okay with the truth that things aren't always perfect or easy. We don't need to pretend it to be that way. We can lean on others. We can accept the help. It doesn't make us less strong. It takes strength to be vulnerable.

TRANSITIONING FROM MOM TO CAREER MOM

A few months later, it was time for me to make the jump from mom to career mom. I was eager to start my professional career as a chiropractor. I wanted to open my own office from the get-go. I approached a massage therapist in town who was established with her business and asked if she would be interested in a partnership. She was happy in her setup and not looking to have anyone join her. No big deal; I moved on to plan B.

I made some calls to chiropractors in neighboring areas to ask about their experience with their communities and opening a practice. Through my conversation with one of the doctors, I was invited to join her in her office two days a week. This would give me the experience of learning from a doc already in practice while not having the business stresses of running my own office. I learned what I wanted and did not want in the office of my dreams one day. I thought about the staff. I thought about the office layout and colors. I thought about who my target market would be. I was enjoying it so much! I accepted that it was okay to learn from someone else. I didn't have to have all the answers to what to do coming out of school. She was helping me. I had the balance of days with my girls and days with my career.

About nine months into this practice arrangement, I got a phone call from the massage therapist I had approached nearly a year before. She was ready and wanted to pursue a partnership. Looking back, it was a bit of a shot in the dark. We didn't know each other, yet we were entering into a relationship as business partners. We opened a new location with build-out expenses and collaborated on decorating the office. We decided to keep two business names with shared overhead expenses and staff. She had the experience of already being open, and I had the drive to make something new and successful. She helped build my business, and I, in turn, helped her. We became great friends, and our business was very successful. It was an unheard-of arrangement in my profession but perfect for our family and for me as a mom trying to get it all done.

GROWING OUR FAMILY

A few years in, and my husband and I were ready to continue growing our family. We once again became pregnant. We had a great home daycare to take care of our two daughters and strong family support to help when needed. My husband was successful in his job and was amazing with our girls on the nights or weekend days when I was trying to grow my practice.

The births of our first two baby girls had been very exciting, and this third daughter did not want to be described as boring. Twenty-two days before my due date, our family was driving to vacation at a cottage up north for the week. While packing, I had luckily had the mother's intuition to pack the baby seat, just in case. Sure enough, an hour into our drive, I could feel my body starting to go into labor. Between my husband insisting that things would settle down once we arrived and my niece telling me how she had watched a movie where a baby was born at Walmart, I really wanted to get to the cottage and put our girls to bed. The minute they were asleep, I let my husband know we had to go to the hospital. A short hour later, we had another baby girl, and our family had grown to five.

I made the phone call to the doctor that would be covering for me to let her know that her start date had moved up three weeks. The plan was for her to take over my practice for six weeks. This would be my mat leave. Many a woman shook their head at me when they heard my plan, thinking it was crazy to take such little time off. I clearly under-stood that the time I would have off with this baby would be short, but never in her life would she have her mom working a forty-hour week.

It didn't matter if this wasn't what was traditional because it wasn't up to everyone else to decide what I do. I am creating my life and what works for me. What I want.

BALANCING MOTHERHOOD AND A BUSINESS

Three children and running a business with my husband working meant we needed more help. We hired a nanny to move in with our family. It was not easy. Remember that I'm not good at being vulnerable. I shouldn't have to ask for help. I should be able to handle it all. I chose to have these children, and I should take care of them. We had judgments from others as to how could we bring someone else in to help raise our children. It was not a simple decision.

Our wonderful nanny arrived, and there was no looking back. This is not to say that it was easy to adapt to. There was another woman in my home. Another woman was going to comfort my girls when they were hurt and I wasn't around. Would they grow to love her more? Would there be a chance they would cry when she left the room? These were valid thoughts that went through my mind. Even when she was part of our home early on, I had my doubts whether it was the right way to go. I had decided that she was there for our girls. I could still handle many of the household chores and take care of my family. The time that she freed up for me with the house chores she did gave me more time in the evenings and weekends to be with my husband and our girls and enjoy the time with them.

My family often recalls how lucky we were to have her in our home; how lucky we were to have someone help us and care for our daughters.

My fear of her replacing me was never rooted in logic. She was a wonderful caregiver, and I was the mom. My girls still came running to greet me when I got home. They still loved my snuggles, and I still had plenty of time with them. The plus side was they had another adult to love them. We were a team. I had come to accept the help and it made everyone's life better.

As my career evolved for the first ten years, my focus was on my family. I loved practice. I had goals, but many of them sat in the back seat to raising my girls. This was difficult in a male-dominated profession where success was often measured by how big your practice was—how many patients you saw in a week and how much money you collected. It can be difficult to not be hitting those markers for success. Did it define my level of success? Or can I define what I want success to look like? Looking back, I know exactly how successful I was.

Success comes in many forms. It is only when we compare ourselves to someone else's success that we may fail to measure up. There is no right way. Knowing the life you want to create and following your path is the right way. Strength is necessary to follow your path. Strength to handle tough situations. Strength to create a family. But strength isn't enough. Strength is not available 100 percent of the time. There is strength in acknowledging that things aren't perfect. There is strength in pivoting and changing course, in asking for help, and in accepting help.

I am a strong woman. I have had a village around me to lift me up my entire life, and this has made me even stronger. I am at a different place in life. There are no little dolls to carry to the store and tuck in at night. My girls are grown and are now in their late teens and early twenties.

They are comfortable in taking on challenges and just as comfortable in asking for help when needed. I admire their ability to do both. My practice is thriving while I take care of moms and their children. I learn from moms every day and share strength by teaching them the importance of taking care of themselves too. That little girl playing with dolls has lived out her dream.

SLEEP IS FOR EVERYONE!

LILY HORBATIUK

LILY HORBATIUK

Lily Horbatiuk is the owner of Lil Baby Sleep and the founder of the Your Dream Plan™ and Lil Potty Plan™. She is a Pediatric Sleep Consultant, Potty Training Consultant, and "Oh Crap" Potty Training Specialist. Lily provides customized support to help parents conquer developmental milestones with ease, while ensuring they are equipped with a step-by-step plan that suits their own unique family needs and comfort.

Website: www.lilbabysleep.com

FB/IG: @lilbabysleep @lilpottyplan

For my Tio Toño, who weaved music and laughter into my life. My biggest role model; my biggest supporter. You will live in everything I do. I know you are singing to me from heaven always. Your Preciosa.

CHAPTER 2

FINDING PURPOSE THROUGH MOTHERHOOD

I have a vivid memory of scoffing at myself when thinking about the possibility of owning my own business one day. As a young adult, I didn't know what I wanted to be, but I clearly knew what I didn't want to become: an entrepreneur. Owning a business seemed like something brave humans do, but I wanted no part in it. I saw the struggle early on and had zero desire for that lifestyle.

I've always thought of myself as ambitious, and I was fairly certain from a young age that what I wanted to do was help people in a deeper life-changing way, to serve and dedicate myself to humanitarian causes. I also knew early on in my career that I loved connecting with people in general. A former manager I worked with said something to me that I remember clearly to this day: "Lily, you have a special ability to connect with people very quickly on a personal and deep level. Hone those soft skills—they are your superpower."

I really like getting to know people, so I knew I could blend my desire to help people with my ability to connect to them. This brought me right to the doorstep of PR, communications, and sales. I studied International Development and worked for a number of nonprofit organizations, on the ground in Peru and South America, and I built partnerships to bring social justice programming into Canadian schools. I then leaned into sales and gained experience working for some of the biggest food companies in the world. I loved the challenge of being in direct sales and getting to know what people really wanted and finding something that matched their needs.

As I got married and settled into family life, I really wasn't sure which way to lean. I certainly didn't think I could do all of it: work for an NGO, work in sales, and now, start a family. You see, I like structure. I like working for someone else. I like making money for the boss and having the security of knowing I will get my trusty salary to bring home. I don't like chaos and uncertainty, and I certainly don't want to work myself into the ground like I've heard business owners often have to do to survive, not to mention succeed!

Nope, nope, *nope*—not for me.

Then came Philip.

POST-BIRTH DIFFICULTIES

Throughout my entire pregnancy, I was told horror stories of what to expect when the baby came. "You will never sleep again!" or the trusty "now you live for your children." To be honest, I was scared and took this as a given. I had chosen to become a mother, so this is what came with it, right?! I accepted it. I was mentally prepared to never sleep again, and I had to *really* try because I love sleep. I've always *loved* sleep. I spend a lot of time talking with people in social settings and need that rest, that silence, that alone time, that mental break.

There were two things that were emphasized throughout our prenatal classes: You will not sleep so "sleep when the baby sleeps," and "you must breastfeed *if* you want to give your baby *the best*." Hell yeah, I do! Okay, so I must do both of those things. I was being erased and my child would now replace me in importance. Cool. Cool.

My son was born two weeks late via C-section. He was perfect. I had my game plan (I love me a good game plan). And then I started to lose control of the game plan.

While spending days recovering from the C-section, I was also desperately trying to latch this baby. Many nurses and lactation consultants came to help me, but it just wasn't happening, so instead of providing me with options, they gave me directions to manually express and feed with a syringe, and he would eventually do it. Off I went home on my own with a tiny little human I had to keep alive.

The next day I noticed my son was warm, and he cried pretty much all night without stopping. I was like, "Yup, just like they told me." But I felt something was off. We took his temperature, and it was high; he had a fever. We rushed him to the hospital, and they let us in right away because of his age. A fever in babies that young is not good. We were put in a room, and the nurses and doctors couldn't find his vein; it was just too small. I hid behind a big machine (I have no recollection of what it was), literally hid and covered my ears while my husband held down our son so they could find a vein to hook him up to an IV. I remember this part vividly because it was the beginning of my feelings of failing as a mother. He was severely dehydrated and had lost a significant amount of body weight.

A nurse snuck in formula for us because it was a "baby-friendly" hospital, which meant formula was discouraged. The nurse had to go to a separate pharmacy to find it and brought it in like contraband. After five days in the hospital and the day before Christmas, we were home. But this was just the beginning. What I did from that day on was punish myself for starving my child. I was failing at this mother thing, and I was going to make it right by sacrificing my entire self and rendering myself invisible, just like society had told me to do up to that point. I would become a martyr.

I started this penance by pumping, feeding, holding, and repeating. These months went on in a blur. At five months, I was still pumping, feeding, holding, and now rocking to sleep. On a good day, I would get maybe a few hours of sleep, but most nights I was up in this cycle of sleep deprivation. The only thing I heard was that this was what "good mothers" did. They sacrificed themselves day and night. "Hang in there," "This will pass," and "Your baby needs you right now." But I kept wondering, where was the village? Was there a number I could call to alert them?

What about me? I dared not express concern for my needs or even think about them. There was no place for that. *It wasn't about me anymore.* I transformed into a different person, someone I no longer recognized. I was resentful, overwhelmed, and couldn't stand the sound of my baby crying. We were both so exhausted that we cried anyway. I developed postpartum anxiety and couldn't step out of my house because of overwhelming fear.

POSTPARTUM ANXIETY

My home became a box of anxiousness and sadness that I could not leave. One day I attempted to drive down the street to the grocery store. It was a cold winter day, and I had never used the brand-new stroller we had bought with the illusion that I would be out for walks and meeting up with friends for coffee or going to the mall for a day of window shopping. Instead, I was fumbling with this stroller in the middle of an empty parking lot. I finally got it adjusted, got the baby in it, then went into the store. I picked up a few things before I felt an overwhelming urge to leave. On the way out, it was snowing. I was already anxious because of the cold, and I put my baby into the car but could not close the stroller. I tried and tried. My hands got shaky and sweaty, and all the worst-case scenarios came rushing to my mind. What if we froze here? What have I done exposing us to this? I was panicking and even tried putting the stroller in the trunk unfolded, but it didn't fit and there was no one around to help. I felt hot tears running down my face. I smacked the stroller, and it closed! Frantically, I got back in the car and rushed home as fast as I could, vowing to never step outside my house again. The world was full of dangers, and my anxiety could not stand the thoughts of what *could* happen.

In the first five months of my son's life, I struggled with two bouts of mastitis, one of which required a hospital visit. After my son's horrific tongue and lip tie release, I continued to pump and try breastfeeding, but I was unsuccessful. Just the thought of breastfeeding brought me to a cold sweat. I was miserable and exhausted and needed to make a change. I needed to sleep. My husband helped a lot; he was always wanting to take over and started taking shifts on weekends. I would pump, prepare a bottle, and go to sleep for a few hours. I knew, however, that we needed help. I started looking online and began learning about sleep. I was shocked that **this didn't have to be my life**. Things could change and improve. Trying to put my baby to sleep was inadvertently keeping us both up and creating stress around it.

HOPE

As I started to learn about sleep, I began feeling hope. I started to implement what I was learning, and although making those changes was difficult, the more I stuck to it, the more sleep I was getting! It was magical. Four hours, then six hours, then twelve hours! I felt the fog lift. I stopped pumping, a decision I felt good about. I became a happier person, which, in turn, made me a happier mom with a lot more patience. I was able to do things like shower, sleep, and go on outings, and surprisingly, my postpartum anxiety improved. I joined mom groups, made friends, and became very active in hosting playdates and organizing walks. When moms came over to my house for playdates, they were shocked by how easily I could walk upstairs and put my baby down for a nap, say good night, sleep tight, and within minutes, have him happily fall asleep. It was a big shift from the shell of a person I had once been. I wanted to tell all moms that they didn't have to be that tired and that what society was telling us was a lie. Sleep deprivation is not a badge of honor to be proud of. It doesn't mean you are a better mother because you are "sacrificing yourself." Women don't have to sacrifice themselves when they become mothers; instead, they have to love themselves more.

I was happy and then I was mad because this idea of selflessness was promoted and prevalent throughout society. The phrase "they need you" made it seem like by putting your child down, you were abandoning them as if you weren't a loving parent, and now I could see that what my baby needed was sleep. And so did I. Our relationship flourished, and I flourished—not only as a mother and wife but also as a person.

I acknowledge that this might not be everyone's journey, but it's a journey that led me to leave my full-time job and become, dare I say it . . . an entrepreneur.

ENTREPRENEURSHIP

I studied hard, went back to being a student, and got certified, twice! Shortly after, I started *Lil Baby Sleep* while my daughter was a newborn. I had a computer in one hand and a baby on my lap. I felt and still feel passionate about helping families feel their best in whatever way that works for them. That passion for helping others pushed me feet first into entrepreneurship, and I had to learn to swim really quickly.

The struggles of entrepreneurship were real and exceeded my expectations. I grasped on for dear life with my passion in one arm and my young family in the other. I was juggling motherhood, entrepreneurship, and now an intensely emotionally involved profession helping tired families who are emotionally and physically drained.

Every day for the first three years of running my business, I faced the questions: Do I go on? Do I continue to move forward, or do I run? Most of the time I wanted to run, but by keeping a clear vision of the purpose of the work I was doing supporting moms, I became *their* village. I had to keep throwing myself into the unknown with the hope of coming out the other side generally unharmed. The more I threw myself into that fear, the more I came out of it with greater determination than before.

My fire for what I do stems from my journey and the ongoing message we as mothers receive about not putting ourselves first. We as mothers are selfish if we put our needs first (like sleep). We as mothers should "sacrifice" ourselves, our identities, our happiness, and our well-being. I say that this is complete bullshit. We need to stop making mothers invisible and put them at the forefront of priorities. **The priority**.

We are inundated with responsibilities, worries, pressures, and the reality of going back to work. The expectations are enormous. We cannot lose ourselves, because if we do, we are not giving our best selves to our children. I know the messaging needs to change. Being a "good mom" means being a **happy mom**. Period.

I work now because I love to work. I have a greater purpose. I want to be a role model to my kids and model how to love oneself first so we can properly help others, rather than being a shell of a person who doesn't recognize herself at all.

The number one thing I want my children to take away is that loving oneself is the best gift you can give to others, but it's also the hardest thing you will do. Going against what society tells us is right is not easy.

Ultimately, though, it offers the best outcomes. I still struggle with this daily. However, the more I work with families, the more I hear how their lives are transformed with our support, the more I see the value in the struggle, and the more I see myself and love myself, my team, and the families that trust us with their sleep.

Lil Baby Sleep now helps thousands of families worldwide get the sleep they need. Sleep is for EVERYONE! It helps mothers feel their best. *Lil Baby Sleep* changes family dynamics and helps guide parents through online programs, both for sleep and potty training. My goal is to be there through all those big milestones that parents struggle with (like the aforementioned sleep and potty training), so they become the least of their worries. At the same time, we change mindsets and improve lives. We have a team of wonderful sleep coaches who truly care and do a happy dance anytime we get a "win" post in our private members' group!

Additionally, I help coach other sleep consultants in my other passion: business and sales. I guide them through this journey of entrepreneurship so they can better serve more families and change lives.

Now when I think of entrepreneurship, I still think it's a struggle, but it's a struggle that is meant to make me a better person; it's a struggle and lifestyle that while difficult (like most things that are worth the results), helps me feel fulfilled and impacts lives. Entrepreneurship found me.

THOSE WORDS WILL NOT DEFINE ME. I REFUSE TO GIVE THEM LIFE. I GET TO CHOOSE.

FRANCES MURRAY

FRANCES MURRAY

Frances Murray is a baker and Food Network competitor. As the owner of Fran Murray Co., a socially conscious boutique gifting agency, she helps businesses show appreciation to their top people by gifting curated experiences with ease. Fran's food artistry has adorned many print and online media sources, including *Huffington Post*, *Toronto Star*, and notable blogs and magazines. When she is not devising plans on how to take over the world, she is either spending time with her family of six or hiding out in the bathroom for ten minutes of peace. It's no joke in these entrepreneur mom streets.

Website: www.franmurray.co

FB/IG: @franmurray.co

For those trying to find their way in a world that has already counted them out.

Remain in motion. I see you. I love you. You belong here.

CHAPTER 3

NO, I GET TO CHOOSE

My earliest memories of trying to figure out who I am and where I fit in started in Kingston, Jamaica. I attended St. George's Girls School, an infant and primary school in downtown Kingston. Our uniform consisted of a green-and-white checkered sleeveless dress, a white collared dress shirt, brown socks, brown shoes, and ribbons for our hair. We were well-dressed children who had social responsibilities. There were rules we had to follow while wearing our school uniform: we were expected to be on our best behavior, both on and off school property. This meant that there was no "ramping" (playing or kidding around) or eating on the road while in uniform. At home, I played with the children of the families who rented rooms close to where we lived. I remember a few times hearing my name called, and I would act like I had "no broughtupsy," which is how Jamaicans refer to someone with bad manners. Kids around me used Jamaican swear words, and they knew I wasn't allowed to. When I did, they would tell on me, as kids do. Those little rascals.

I recall one incident where I swore like the rest of them. One of the children ran to my dad to tell him what I said. Lucky for me, only my dad was home. Phew! Jamaican moms do not play—they whip you first and don't even ask questions later. My dad thought I could do no wrong, which I absolutely loved. He ran her away and said, "My daughter would never say something like that." Yup, I was Daddy's girl. And yes, I was that kid who knew her parents would defend her. So, again at home, I had to be set apart. I didn't quite fit in with my friends because I couldn't act or speak like them. My behavior was different. I learned I couldn't follow the crowd. I couldn't take part in what everyone else was doing because my path, the expectations of me, wouldn't allow it.

JOURNEY INTO ENTREPRENEURSHIP

Unbeknownst to me, my journey into entrepreneurship started early. I remember cutting paper into asymmetrical pieces and walking around to the machine operators at a uniform manufacturer located in Kingston and where my mom worked as an office manager. I sold these hideous looking craft cutouts, or "fish eggs" as I called them. Almost every day I saw people selling items on the roadside, so like the imitator I was, I wanted to sell some of my own! After all, I had a whole factory full of people to sell them to. Genius move, if you ask me. Picture a skinny little girl with bright brown eyes who everyone called "Mousey." I was the factory mouse . . . the only kid bouncing around and popping out of everywhere, and I mean everywhere. There was no corner I didn't visit and no one I didn't talk to. Everyone knew me, and I knew everyone. When Friday came around, I would collect payment for my "fish egg" deliveries made earlier in the week.

When the news broke that I was going to be heading to "farin" (what Jamaicans refer to as overseas), it was all my "fish egg" clients would talk about. I knew it was where my aunts, who had visited us a few times prior, lived, but I knew very little about it. My mom told me the place was called Toronto. My clients told me it was very cold and snowy, and I would have to wear a lot of clothes. I couldn't imagine wearing a lot of clothes. Most of my wardrobe fit in one drawer, and my school clothes were hung up on a nail on a wall adjacent to our bed. I literally only owned one pair of pants, which I hardly ever wore, for crying out loud.

I had never seen snow before. The most ice I had ever seen was in Sky Juice carts and in fish stalls at the market. I imagined a place that was cold and dark with big single-level homes and yellow lights shining through the windows. I also thought everyone had chimneys; after all, the homes on postcards had chimneys. I also thought that fish fell from the sky when it snowed! I am sure the fish market had something to do with my association of an obscene amount of ice and fish. I was nine, so I knew that fish lived in water (given that I lived on an island and went to the beach enough times). Therefore, they must only fall from the sky in farin!

MOVING TO TORONTO

It was the day of the big trip! My mom dressed me in the cutest deep purple dress. There I was with my mom, dad, and brother on the way to the plane. We got to the airport, and as we approached the plane outside on the tarmac, we stopped. My mom and dad kissed. I mean, they really kissed. Like, a long, long, long kiss. I knew then that he wasn't coming to Canada with us, but I hardly internalized it because I was so eager to see how the inside of that airplane looked. I said goodbye to my dad and eagerly followed my mom up the stairs. I had no idea what the plane ride would be like. I fastened my seatbelt, and the plane started moving faster and faster. My stomach felt like it did during roller coaster rides at Coney Island! I had no idea what was going on and panicked in silence. Finally, it stopped.

We arrived in Toronto on September 1, 1991. We were met at the airport by people I was told were family members. Toronto was not what I imagined. The houses in our neighborhood weren't one level—they were tall. And it didn't even snow all the time. It was very warm outside, and to my surprise, it wasn't always dark. We were welcomed with open arms by my extended family and, oh boy, were there a lot of them.

We went to my aunt's farm where we spent lots of weekends and holidays. I shared a room with one of my younger cousins. The room was opposite the room my mom slept in. One early evening, I met my mom in the upstairs hallway as she was coming out of the bathroom that was sandwiched between our rooms. I asked, "Mommy, when are we going back home?"

My mom responded, "We are home."

I don't have any other memories of that evening, but I am sure I cried myself to sleep. I missed my dad. I realized then that this wasn't a trip; it was permanent. For whatever reason, I had never attached permanency to this trip to Toronto.

SCHOOL DAYS

I was enrolled in grade 5 that September. While I don't recall feeling like I was the minority, as I did not yet have that word in my vocabulary, I do recall finding it odd that white people outnumbered black people. Back home, I had never experienced being in a room or any building where that was the case. I was used to my teachers being black, principals being black, business owners being black, bank workers being black, people in every profession being black. And now, there weren't very many. At nine years old, I was realizing the life I once knew and loved was no longer. What now?

In our home, my much older cousin, who I called Aunt, was a stickler for academics. She wanted us kids to strive for excellence in everything we did. I remember accompanying her to parent–teacher interviews and overhearing her talking to the teachers. She asked for us to get extra work and for the teachers to push us to do our very best. There was a critique or two of their teaching abilities thrown in as well! I knew this was her expectation, and I wanted to live up to it. We kids were even enrolled in Saturday classes at a learning institute and were those teachers ever strict! My heart skipped a beat whenever I walked into the building, which was a house converted into a school. I recall one day when I forgot my homework and someone had to drive home to get it. I got in so much trouble that day; I honestly thought my heart was going to come right out of my chest the way it was beating so fast and hard. I learned at this age to color within the lines, do what I was told, do what was expected of me first, and then have fun. Our household wasn't super strict, but there were expectations we had to live up to, and as long as we did our schoolwork and got good grades, which we always did, we could have fun.

In high school, I had to do research for an essay I had to write. This was around the time when reports of black men being pulled over by police at a disproportionate rate than non-black men were being broadcasted all over the news. My essay had to do with racial profiling, so I went to the library to find some data. I came across a book that had some good information I could use, or so I thought, until I read predictions it had for my future. According to the statistics in the book, black females from single parent homes were more likely to have children at a young age out of wedlock and live in poverty. I was shocked and appalled. I had no idea prior to reading those statistics that my family dynamic was considered an impediment to me. After all, I was surrounded by so much love. My mom told me every chance she got that I could be anything I wanted to be. She affirmed me. This book expected the opposite of me. Nope. Not a chance. I told myself I would not become a statistic. From that day forward, the lessons I learned about striving for excellence and doing my best every time cemented in my psyche and became my driving force. I repeated to myself, "Those words will not define me. I refuse to give them life. I get to choose."

From then on, I made the decision to curate a life where I would get married before having children, and I would carve out a living for myself. I continued to color within the lines all throughout high school. I went to university, not because I had the means (because I didn't), but because it was expected of me. I also wanted to prove those statistics wrong. I graduated, I got married and had kids, and I had a career I was advancing in. I turned my passion for baking into a side hustle. Yes! I made it! I did it! I did what I was told. I colored within the lines. I beat the statistics. I curated the "perfect" life. I won! Or so I thought.

BECOMING AUTHENTICALLY ME

One day in January 2017, I woke up and realized that all the stuff I didn't have time to address when I was busy achieving, all the stuff I had placed in boxes with pretty bows, fell off their shelves and opened up. Everything was exposed, and I didn't know which stuff went into which box. It was a mess. I didn't know where to start. I felt as if I had been asleep for the previous ten years, then woke up and couldn't remember how I got here, to this place: married, home, children. It wasn't that "here" was a bad place, it was that I couldn't remember the journey. I was forced to sit with my stuff. Analyze my stuff. I was forced to explore issues with vulnerability, repressed memories, fatherlessness, self-worth, and belonging. I had to do the hard work to figure it out. No one could help me because I didn't have the words to explain what I was going through. If I asked for help, I would run the risk of being judged or being told I should be happy with the life I had. I remember wondering why I felt such discontent. I should've been happy. Happiness is a choice. I knew that. I chose it. But I didn't feel it. Where was the symptom of my happiness? Where did it go?

I had been so caught up with proving those stats wrong. I realized that through the years, I had cloned traits of people I either admired or whom I thought I should emulate. I lost who I was. This drive, this yearning to strive forward and excel, was not about believing I was worthy of the accomplishments but rather about disproving stereotypes. I had to find the real Fran and give her permission to show up authentically so she could impact the people assigned to her sphere of influence.

During my career in corporate, I felt a bit out of place during a few off-site meetings and networking / social events. I was good at what I did, of course, but I was bothered by corporate politics, the boys' club culture, and a less-than-desirable corporate culture. As my zeal faded, I withdrew into myself, my circle became smaller, and my tolerance for people and their shenanigans took a sharp decline. I was bothered that I would go to fancy dinners with people who had no interest in me and with whom I had no interest in. I would attend breakfast meetings in rooms of hundreds of people and maybe see a handful of people who looked like me. I felt like I didn't belong. I couldn't find my place. I wanted to fit in, but I wasn't willing to pay the price of compromising who I was.

I spent many years trying to find my place within the baking industry. I knew I didn't want a bakery because I figured that running it would be like another job. I would have to be somewhere by a certain time and close by a certain time, etc. No thanks. I wasn't quite sure how to niche down without confining my creativity, so I did a bit of everything. I did dessert tables for a while, which is basically an assortment of pretty-looking desserts designed on a table. I didn't like the fact that too many of my clients cared less about the flavors of the desserts and more about the aesthetics. I am a baker, so the flavor is paramount with the aesthetics being an awesome second. I ventured into baking wedding cakes. Again, I was competing with bakers who used bucket mixes and fillings and such, something I could not bring myself to do. Why? I am a *baker*. Baking from scratch and flavor profiling is my jam! I was great at decorating wedding cakes; however, I would cringe every time a bride would ask for vanilla or chocolate. It was like a dagger to the heart. I recall someone looking at me like I had two heads when I passionately explained the possibilities of the flavor profile of their cake.

Despite my work being featured in magazines and blogs, I was tired of trying to fit in. I knew I was struggling with this for a reason, but I couldn't figure out why. I wanted to belong, but I didn't. I tried to fit in, but I couldn't—I didn't feel as if I had found my place—a place that resonated with my soul. I remember feeling like my business was separate from me and being exhausted from consciously trying to separate the two.

When the opportunity came for me to go full time in my business, I was ready to infuse all of myself. I said yes to me! This was my opportunity to leap, and I took it. I made the decision to pivot to e-commerce and launched a few product lines during the pandemic. I surrounded myself with ambitious, like-minded entrepreneurs. I learned that I had everything I needed to succeed, and that my success is dependent on building one relationship at a time. I turned inward and started nurturing relationships with people who love what I do and how I do it. This decision opened up a series of networks I never imagined and opportunities I never thought possible.

The pandemic gave me the space to truly see the version of me that my journey toward authenticity was revealing. And you know what? I fell in love with her. I am enamored by her. This person who I am becoming is incredible. She is grounded. She is loving. She is inspiring. She is captivating. She is fierce. She is a ray of sunshine. She is a safe place for people to show up as their authentic selves. The most amazing part is, she is just getting started.

I was introduced to her when I gave myself permission to be. Permission to dream big without knowing the how. Permission to love on herself. Permission to seek out for herself what she needs to strive, as opposed to hoping someone would see her and lend her a hand. I found my wings. I started raising my hand. I purposely showed up in spaces I was uncomfortable being in, just so I would learn how to be content in uncomfortable spaces.

No longer was I swimming upstream trying to prove anything to anyone or trying to live up to others' expectations of me or trying to fit in. I was living for me. I was swimming in my own stream. I was demystifying and disrupting what success means to me, what a "good wife" means to me, and what a "good friend" means to me. I curated my world and gave myself permission to belong. I chose me, loved me, and I saw me. I told myself that I matter, and I believe it. I belong here, am loved here, and am seen here. I matter here.

You matter here.

Today, I live in the Greater Toronto Area with my husband with whom I am jointly funding the social lives of our four jobless kids (ages 2 to 10)! Our home is loud and action-packed when they are awake and incredibly peaceful when they are asleep. I am loved for the amazing and not so amazing parts of me. My circle is small on purpose, and I surround myself with people whose eyes light up when I enter the room.

I am also the proud owner of *Fran Murray Co.*—a socially conscious boutique gifting agency aimed at helping busy entrepreneurs and companies nurture key relationships through curated giftings. Our gifting options include gourmet dessert products made in house by my company, as well as products made in small businesses owned by women or people of color. Growing a business within a space where profit meets philanthropy is a responsibility I am blessed to have been bestowed. Everyone deserves to be loved, seen, and appreciated. I am on a mission to help the world put this belief into action, one relationship at a time.

I celebrate in advance what lies ahead of my journey to becoming authentically me.

YOU, TOO,
CAN TURN
WHATEVER
YOU'RE GOING
THROUGH INTO
SOMETHING
BEAUTIFUL.

LAURA ENGEN

LAURA ENGEN

Laura Engen is the owner and lead designer of Laura Engen Interior Design, a full-service residential interior design studio based in Minneapolis/St. Paul, Minnesota. Laura believes that design is more than a look, it's about creating an environment that allows you to live with function and style. Laura lives with her husband, their two boys, and their dog in their beloved fixer-upper. When she's not working on her clients' homes, you can find her going on family walks or working on the latest project around the house.

Website: www.lauraengen.com

FB/IG: @lauraengenid

To my loving husband and our beautiful children. And to all the mothers and those who want to be a mother, you're not alone.

CHAPTER 4

CHASING MOTHERHOOD DREAMS AND BUSINESS SUCCESS

Our fertility story started when I was twenty-seven. I was newly married, and I had just begun a new job after working for the same interior designer for more than six years. The job wasn't working out, something I felt in my gut. At first, I thought I needed a little more time to figure out how things were done, but there was more going on beneath the surface.

As all of this was happening, I felt an urge to start a family. I was frustrated and confused. We had agreed we were going to wait a few years after we got married to start trying for a baby so we could focus on our careers and traveling. But every time I saw a baby or a commercial for a box of diapers, I broke down crying. It was a sign, and it was loud and clear. I wanted a baby, and I didn't want to wait.

After talking it through with my husband, we decided I was going to quit my job and start my own business. In March 2013, my first baby was born—my business: *Laura Engen Interior Design*. I had almost no savings, no business degree, and no clients, but for some reason, none of that scared me because I knew I already had everything I needed to run a successful business.

We got pregnant five months into starting this business. We were thrilled, but we were also just barely scraping by. I was twenty-eight years old when our first son was born. He came two days early, so it was a bit of a surprise. As I was lying in the hospital bed between contractions that day, I realized one of my clients had a custom sofa being delivered the next morning, and I had been planning to meet the delivery people at the house. It was my first custom furniture order, and I was so disappointed I wasn't going to be there for the delivery. I remember sending an email from my phone to the client and the delivery company late that night about my situation and wished them well. It was my first reality check of how life as a mom and a business owner would look. After thirty-six hours of labor, I was exhausted and nothing was working, so we had an emergency C-section, and our son was born. He was perfect.

A few weeks later, I got my first call from a contractor. He started our conversation by asking how we were doing, then said, "I know you just had a baby, but I need your help." Now, I'm guessing that any reasonable person would say, "I'd love to, but I just had a baby, and now is not a good time." But I needed the money, so I said yes. However, we had another problem. I couldn't be gone for more than two to three hours at a time because I was breastfeeding. My husband had to drive me to some of those appointments early on so I could nurse right before I went into the meeting and nurse in the car as soon as the meeting was done. My whole day revolved around feeding times.

THE BALANCING ACT

After five months of juggling work and being a full-time stay-at-home mom, I knew I needed to get serious about finding childcare so I could return to work on a regular basis. I loved being home, but I really loved my work and wanted to have dedicated work hours. We found a daycare that was available three days a week, so my husband and I each took a day off to make it work. I remember going into the office and being so productive; I felt like a superhuman, powering through tasks without worrying about nursing or naptimes. And something magical happened that I didn't expect. I thought I'd be worried about the baby all day and that I'd be watching the clock and counting down the minutes until it was time to pick him up at daycare. But to my surprise, when I got to the office, I was focused on my work and excited to be there. Being a designer is so much a part of who I am; I crave that creativity and interaction with my clients. I never felt guilty or torn between the two—my family will always come first, but I needed to work to feel fulfilled. My career is a part of who I am.

Right before our son's first birthday, I started feeling the familiar urge to have a baby again. We waited exactly one year before we started trying, and we were pregnant after the first month. I wanted to be thrilled, but I was so angry. I wanted more time with my baby: he was only a year old, and I had fully expected it would take us months to get pregnant. I had just returned to work, and I was really getting in the flow of things again. After getting over the initial anger of being pregnant again so soon, I quickly fell in love with our baby-to-be and relished in the familiar feeling of someone moving in my belly and craving the weirdest foods, like steamed green beans with toasted almonds and scrambled eggs for breakfast every morning.

I was thirty years old when it was time for our second son to be born. We arrived at the hospital at our scheduled time for a planned C-section. I remember walking into the operating room and getting on the table and thinking how it felt like I was going into a routine doctor checkup, not preparing to have a baby. When he was born, we were immediately in love.

By this time, I was three years into my business, and the clients had kept coming, regardless of my pregnancy status. It was hard to turn away the work. After our second son was born, I returned to work within a month, taking on small projects like paint consultations and doing furniture layouts. I didn't know how to say no, which was a real problem for me. I can remember making promises to clients that I'd have the work done within a few days or a week, thinking I could power through, but I would end up disappointing the client. Having a toddler and a newborn at home plus running a business was the most challenging time of my life.

Eventually, we were able to get our youngest into the same daycare as our eldest son, and I was once again back at the office conquering tasks faster than ever, determined to get my work done so I could enjoy family time at home. As much as I enjoyed having an office where I could escape, we were really struggling to get by. We had two kids in daycare (which cost more than double our mortgage), I was paying rent for an office, and I was trying to pay myself a livable wage. I was spending over an hour in the car commuting, time I could have spent with my family. It was all too much, so I moved my office home into our tiny house to save money and spend more time with my kids.

THE FIXER-UPPER

By the time the kids were two and four years old, I was ready to move. We stumbled on our dream fixer-upper house; it was on the same street as the kids' daycare and just a block away. It had been on the market for a long time, and I imagine no one had snatched it up because it required so much work. As a designer, I saw the potential. Our first offer was turned down, and so were our second and third offers. After several months of back-and-forth with the owner, we took a gamble and sold our house, made our final offer, and got our dream home.

From the moment we moved into our new home, it was under construction in one form or another, but we were the ones doing the work. I was always painting something, ripping up carpet or tile floors, changing out ugly light fixtures, or building cabinets. I still wonder where I found the energy to get all those projects done while raising two toddlers and running a business that was financially supporting our family.

Once we were in our new house, I began feeling that urge again to have a baby. If I'm being totally honest, I don't know that the urge ever really went away, but we were trying to be financially responsible. I told my husband that I was ready, and while he was less than thrilled, he knew it was only a matter of time because he knew I wanted a big family. So,

I devised a plan so we could make it work. Now all we had to do was get pregnant, which I thought was the easy part.

OUR FERTILITY JOURNEY

After nearly one year of trying, and at the age of thirty-three, I was pregnant! I was beyond thrilled. Then several weeks later, I woke up with light spotting. By dinner time, I was bleeding more heavily and felt so sick that I had to lie down. I knew something was wrong. I knew I wasn't pregnant anymore. We had had our first miscarriage.

It was around this time that I realized I needed help, so I found a therapist. I needed someone outside of my family to talk to. Getting pregnant and staying pregnant was proving harder than I thought. We spent our time together talking about my business, pregnancy, and how my personal feelings and emotions were affecting my work. It was extremely helpful to have someone point out when I was being too hard on myself and the ways in which I could improve.

Seven months later we found out that we were pregnant again! I didn't believe it, so I took three tests just to confirm I wasn't imagining it. Then one morning the cramping started, followed by heavy bleeding, so I decided to work from the living room sofa that day. By mid-morning I was in the most excruciating pain, and I knew I was no longer pregnant. This is when I realized that I may be having an ectopic pregnancy.

I called the doctor's office, explained my symptoms, and drove myself to the appointment. The ultrasound revealed I was not pregnant, but I did have some bleeding in my abdomen, and I needed surgery. After waking up from surgery, they told me that my right fallopian tube had ruptured. It was beyond repair, so they had to remove it. But not to worry, they said, because I could still get pregnant with one tube.

It was the middle of the week, and luckily, I didn't have any appointments that day, as my mind couldn't have been further from work. When you own a business, you're constantly thinking about your calendar, your clients' needs, and how you're communicating with them. Your success revolves around it. I had never been in a situation like this, and I didn't know how to handle my emotions and my recovery in a professional manner. Should I cancel meetings and give myself time to recover? Would my clients be upset? What would I tell them and how much should I tell them about my situation? It was so devastating and personal, and I didn't want my clients to know what was going on. So, I chose to ignore it and move on like nothing ever happened, which was a mistake.

Two days later, I had a photo shoot scheduled for work for one of my latest projects. Interior design is often thought of as glamorous work, but no one tells you how physical it is. I wish I would have recognized that I needed to heal and take care of myself, but I was trying to be strong and return to work. I had lifting restrictions post-surgery, so I called my mom for help with the photo shoot since I knew lifting heavy items was required. After spending two days staging and shooting this project, my body was done. I had developed a fever, and I was having chest pains. I slept the entire weekend just to get back on my feet.

Ten months later, we were pregnant again. I immediately called my doctor to make a plan, as I knew I was at high risk of having another ectopic pregnancy. The first appointment went well, but within a few days, I was experiencing that familiar pain again, but this time on my left side. I knew exactly what was happening. I called the nurse line, and they told me to go to the emergency room right away. After coming out of surgery, they confirmed what I already knew: I had had an ectopic pregnancy on my left side and my tube had ruptured. But there was still hope. They said I was a great candidate for IVF if I still wanted to get pregnant.

I spent those first few weeks after my surgery staring out the window and wondering how I was going to recover, not just physically but emotionally. I was depressed and felt no desire to work or take care of my family. My husband stepped up and took care of the kids so I could rest, and luckily, I had hired a virtual assistant who I let know what happened so she could monitor my inbox and reschedule appointments. I took the next few weeks to recover and give myself space to heal. Accepting help and letting myself rest were the greatest things I could have done for myself.

After the initial depression wore off, we decided to try IVF. I wasn't ready to give up yet. I was thirty-five years old at the time, and my fertility clock was ticking. We had a long road ahead of us, and we had no idea what an emotional roller coaster it would be for our relationship, our family, and the business. We decided to do a program that covered three rounds of IVF, which would give us a better chance of getting pregnant.

Our first round didn't go as planned. I got COVID-19 just as we were about to start and had to wait. Then our egg retrieval had disappointing results, leaving us with only one egg (not the ten to fifteen we were expecting). We proceeded with the transfer, and ten days later found out we were not successful. I knew this was a possibility, so I had a chilled bottle of Chardonnay waiting for me in case I needed help processing the news. I got off the phone with the nurse, poured myself a glass of wine, then went back to my desk in our home office and cried. I felt like my whole world was falling apart yet again. We had lost our baby.

FOCUSING ON WORK

By now, I had been working with a therapist for about a year, but I felt like I needed more support in my business. This is when I enlisted the help of a business coach, Lianne Kim. I had taken the business as far as I could, but I was falling out of love with my work. I was juggling doctor appointments, fertility drug schedules, being a mom, running a household, and trying to grow a thriving interior design business during a global pandemic. I was completely overwhelmed. But just like having a baby, I wasn't ready to give up. I knew I just needed the right people to help me succeed, so I reached out to Lianne, and we began our work together pretty quickly. She helped me see how much I was shouldering on my own and how I needed to think less like a worker bee and more like a CEO.

Through our business coaching work, we did exercises that allowed me the space to envision what my life could look like five years from now and imagine every single detail exactly the way I wanted it to be. I didn't have to worry about the how or why just yet; I could really let go of what was going on in my current life and imagine the outcomes I truly desired. We developed strategies that I could implement right away, including hiring more help so I could get back to doing what I loved. We talked about raising my rates and focusing on working with my dream clients so I could live the lifestyle I desired. I had to learn how to say no, and to my surprise, it felt really good—empowering actually. Investing in coaching saved my business and gave me a sense of purpose again.

CONTINUING IVF

After our first round of IVF, our doctor wanted us to go immediately into our next round. I went in with high hopes that we had adjusted the medications just right and we'd have more success. It was time for our pregnancy test again. I was trying not to be overly optimistic, as I remembered how crushed I had been the last time. I cautiously let myself get excited about the possibility of being a mother again, but later that day I got the call that we were not pregnant.

The next month we had a phone call with the doctor to discuss our next steps. We had to decide whether we wanted to discontinue the program or try again. He said if we weren't successful this time, he would not recommend doing IVF again. I was determined to see it through and decided to try one last time. We agreed it would be best to take some time off to give my body a break from all the medications. We'd try again later in the year.

It's now been over a year since we first started IVF, and I'm currently undergoing our third and final round. By the time this book goes to print, we'll know if we're going to have our baby or if this chapter of our life is closed for good. Either way, I have something to look forward to. I'm becoming the best version of myself, and I wouldn't be here if I hadn't learned to ask for help along the way. Throughout our fertility journey, I found a therapist who has been there to listen and advise me every step of the way, and I enlisted a business coach to help me fall in love with my business again. I was able to turn tragedy into beauty, and my hope in sharing this is if you also are in a season of waiting, you will realize that you, too, can turn whatever you're going through into something beautiful.

I WAS GOING TO BE ALONE—ALONE IN MY GRIEF BECAUSE IN MY MIND I THOUGHT, *THIS IS WHAT STRONG GIRLS DO.* THEY SUFFER IN SILENCE. THEY DON'T NEED ANYONE ELSE. THEY CAN DO IT ALONE. AND LET ME TELL YOU . . . I WAS WRONG.

AMANDA CASINHA

AMANDA CASINHA

Amanda Casinha is the founder of Grind Social Media + Co., a full-service digital marketing agency that focuses on content that converts. After building a seven-figure business in her twenties, she is now passionate about using her 15+ years in marketing to help other businesses grow online. When she isn't creating viral content for her clients, you can find her drinking coffee and listening to true crime podcasts! She lives in Toronto with her husband and two beautiful daughters.

Website: www.grindsocialmedia.com

FB/IG: @ThatTorontoMom @GrindSocialMedia

To my mom, for teaching me empathy. To my girls, for teaching me unconditional love. And to my past, current, and future self, for never giving up.

CHAPTER 5

GROWING THROUGH GRIEF

I was nineteen years old when I became a statistic. I became part of a club that I never asked to join when my mother chose to end her life. And while this story, my story, is full of extreme sadness, grief, and regret, it is also filled with immense resilience, perseverance, and a life that wouldn't have been realized unless I went through this trauma.

On May 23, 2005, my life's trajectory changed. My mother was gone. We were gathered by her side at the hospital, hoping and wishing for a miracle, but it was too late. They could do no more. The machines stopped. We were told to go home. At that moment, the world felt like it had ended. I ran down the hall, crying, screaming, wanting to be alone. And at that moment, I decided that's exactly what I was going to do: I was going to be alone—alone in my grief, because in my mind I thought, *this is what strong girls do*. They suffer in silence. They don't need anyone else. They can do it alone.

And let me tell you . . . I was wrong.

THE EARLY DAYS OF GRIEF

Not too long before my mother died, we were sitting in the kitchen talking about my future. Where I saw myself, would I like to be married, did I want kids? We talked about everything—sex, drugs, boys, everything—my mom was the person to confide in. The parent in the neighborhood that all the kids went to for advice and could talk to without ever feeling judged.

In that conversation, she said one thing that made me look at the way I did things differently: don't ever rely on a person financially; go build something in case you ever have to walk away, then you can. What I didn't realize until recently was that I took those words and turned them into the next fifteen years of my life. Building businesses, not relying on anyone.

The week after my mother passed was a blur. At the time, it felt like the intense pain in my chest, the sleepless nights, and the insufferable loneliness would never end. We had a funeral to plan, and I had a eulogy to write. It felt like an out-of-body experience, or a movie that I was wishing would end but that I couldn't shut off. At the funeral home, I couldn't sit still. I got food for everyone, and I stood outside with friends and family and pretended like everything was okay. They couldn't see me cry; I was strong.

Once the funeral was over, I didn't stay with my family. I escaped back to university, more than 300 miles away from home. I had to finish my degree; I had to act like my mother hadn't just died by suicide. For the next two years, I pretended like everything was okay, but inside, I was a shell of myself. Completely lost, going to class, studying late into the night, partying with friends, and working a full-time job. I did everything and anything to avoid feeling, to avoid having to face the reality that I was now a motherless daughter.

When people asked how I was doing, my response was this: "Shit happens." Yes, I legitimately said that to anyone who asked. In hindsight, I wish someone had just shaken me and told me that it's okay to just grieve—to be sad, cry, scream. But no one did because what do you say to someone who just lost their mother to suicide? It wasn't your typical death. No one we knew had taken their own life. Thus, no one said anything until I gave myself permission to feel.

I did a really good job at keeping everything buried deep within me. I didn't cry and I didn't get angry; I was faking a form of happiness that was acceptable to society. I kept people at an arm's length in fear that if someone got close to me, I would need to feel. I was seen as cold, a bitch. But I was a little girl hiding inside of herself who just wanted her mom to hold her and tell her it was going to be okay.

But my life went on. No one tells you how hard it is to run a business. No one tells you how hard it is to run a business as a young female entrepreneur. No one tells you how hard it is to keep clients happy, do the hiring, keep up with team development and leadership, manage that team and keep them motivated, create content, run reports, be the strategic planner, and on and on. No one tells you all this: you have to learn it; you have to fail at it—and oh did I fail! But then you grow, and you see all that hard work come to fruition, and you look back and realize that every moment, every tear, every doubt was worth it.

And then there's this fact: no one tells you what doing all that work is like after losing your mother to suicide. I once had someone say that they didn't know how I did it all. The truth is, I didn't know how I was doing it all. I was surviving. From the outside, I had everything—a loving relationship, a successful business, a great social life. The truth, though, was that the business was rocky, it took a lot of sleepless weeks (not nights) to get it to where it needed to be, my relationships were struggling because I was not allowing anyone in, and my social life was to mask the deep depression I was experiencing.

But I got up, went to work, hired, trained, taught, led, sold, and gave my everything to build something outside of myself. In hindsight, it wasn't healthy at all, but I just kept going. I had a goal: to be financially independent and to make a name for myself. To be somebody.

And then one day it all fell apart. I was at work, feeling great, and then it hit me—the impending wave of grief (I have coined these as grief spasms)—they come out of nowhere. A sound, a smell, a voice, a phrase—anything can trigger them. And when these spasms hit, they don't care where you are, who you are with, or what you are doing. It is an overwhelming wave of pain, sadness, and loss of breath, and at that moment, blinded by tears, I ran to my car, and I cried. For the first time in two years, I finally cried. It was one of those ugly cries, one that is a deep roaring and soul-crushing cry from the depth of your belly.

After picking myself up, I decided to call a therapist that had been rec-ommended to me years before. That is the moment my life changed. I gave myself permission to grieve, to live a fulfilled life, to feel. To stop being "strong."

THE JOURNEY

The moment I walked into my first therapy appointment, I wanted to run. The idea of having to talk about the pain, anger, and sadness I had hidden within me was more than scary: it made me want to disappear. Because at that moment, I knew what was going to happen—I had to accept that my mother was gone. I had committed to going to that session, just to see what it was all about. What I didn't know was that I would continue to be in therapy for most of my twenties.

At the time my therapy began, I was working my first business, one that went on to become very successful. What I learned through grief therapy was that I had taken everything that my mother had ever said to me and about me and internalized it in such a way that I had to live it out. *You're a strong girl. You don't need to rely on anyone. You are smart. You are going to do big things one day.*

I was working so hard. I was putting in sixty to seventy hours a week leading a team of women to be their best selves for the clients. I was also creating educational content, hiring, firing, leading team meetings, creating marketing plans, and doing long-term strategic planning. My team was everything. I spent countless hours reading leadership books and developing manuals to help them learn as efficiently as possible how to deliver our services to clients. Knowing that I was responsible for the income of these women and the dreams they had was overwhelming, and I had to keep moving forward and pushing them to realize how incredible they actually were.

I was becoming worn out. Being the client-facing person in this business was exhausting. I had to constantly ensure that every person was happy and that the services delivered were of the highest quality so that we could grow further. My days turned into nights—every second of my life was dedicated to running this business and making it successful.

Meanwhile, I was also doubting myself as a leader, grieving the loss of my mother, planning a wedding, and dealing with infertility, but I continued to keep everything inside. I only spoke to my therapist. I didn't want to, or couldn't, speak to others about what I was going through. My friends and family tried, and I struggled to speak the grief out loud. Then I started volunteering as a grief/lay counselor for other suicide loss survivors. That's when I got it. I had to share my story because there were a lot of other people out there just like me. I learned I wasn't alone.

HEALING

For the next nine years, I sat with dozens of people in a one-on-one setting and in group sessions as they shared stories of their loved ones lost to suicide. I led group sessions that had some of the most profound life lessons others had learned. I sat with them in their pain, listened, took it all in, and I shared. It was amazing.

During this time, I truly found healing, and I started to let people in. What my mother had taught me was empathy—being able to sit with someone and not judge, just be—was the greatest gift she gave me and the one that ultimately brought me the success I have today.

Because of the stories of loss from others, I learned I needed to lean on people, that I could no longer go through life alone. It was okay to ask for help. It was okay to be, dare I say it—*vulnerable*.

And then, just when I thought I had a handle on my grief, all the tools in the box, the supports in place, I got married, had kids, and the anger and sadness came rushing back. There are moments in a woman's life when she needs her mom. These were those moments, and she wasn't there. She didn't get to witness me marry my best friend; she never even got to meet him. She didn't get to celebrate when we found out I was pregnant after a long battle with infertility, she wasn't with me at the birth of my children, and I couldn't call her when I was doubting motherhood. I still can't.

Watching all my friends lean on their mothers at a time when I needed mine was probably the hardest part of adulthood so far. I've had to parent myself, trust myself in big life decisions, and hope that what I choose is the right thing to do.

When people say you'll get over it, it's not true. You do not get over it: you get *through* it. And that's what I did, and what I will continue to do. When I realized I no longer had to go at it alone and could trust the people that were there all along, I began to live.

GROWING FROM MISTAKES

For a long time, I thought all that people needed to know about me was that my mother died by suicide. I feared this one sentence was going to define my life, and I didn't want it to, so I pushed it away for as long as I could so that no one could define me that way. I pushed it away so that not even I could define myself that way.

I operated my first business from a place of stoicism, with no room for emotions. I let relationships spoil because of selfishness; I thought my problems were bigger than theirs. When you lose a parent to suicide, the small trivial things don't matter anymore, but these things still mattered to others. I had to learn this the hard way. Instead of saying, "I don't have the capacity for this conversation right now," I would simply just get angry or walk away, never to return. I know better now. I know my limits, and I have learned to set healthy boundaries.

I was loud and my point was known because inside there was a silence that made me want to be heard. I made a lot of mistakes in my twenties, but it was in these mistakes and failures that I learned the biggest lessons. Let's be honest, though; I still have a larger-than-life personality, and I don't truly think I can tone down my voice, but what I have learned is I can create space for others, and I don't have to be the first to speak in every situation.

Today, I am proud to be the owner of *Grind Social Media + Co.*, a successful social media agency. I wouldn't be here today living in Europe with my family, traveling every week and leading a life that I only dreamed about as a young entrepreneur if it weren't for all the lessons learned in the last two decades. I now lead a small but powerful team of women who work together to help other businesses grow online. We help our clients realize their goals and dreams—work that is challenging and rewarding. My days are filled with content creation, strategy, coaching calls, email campaigns, and showing up publicly on social media to build a community. And it is by showing up online, speaking about my expertise, proving it with client success stories, and using social media as my main tool to reach my clients that is bringing me the success I have today.

LESSONS LEARNED

When I lost my mom to suicide, I didn't get an answer as to why. There was no note; there was no goodbye. In retrospect, I have always needed to know everything since that day. I wanted to have the answers and to be the first to know it all. What I've learned today is I don't always need to have the answers, and that's okay.

When I look back at the day my mother told me to make something of myself and to not rely on others for my success—I really ran with it. I tried to do it all on my own, and I was successful, but damn, it's way more fun with people in your corner lifting you up and supporting you. I now know that business can be emotional. It can be raw and real and fun and inspiring, and you can do it all with the help of others. *Community over everything.* I operate from this place now. Be kind, help others, and allow space for others to be seen and heard. Make space for relationships with purpose and intent.

I don't believe in regrets; I believe in lessons learned. If I could go back and speak to my twenty-four-year-old self, I would tell her to slow down. I would tell her not to worry if everything isn't perfect because everything will work out. The business I have today would not exist if I hadn't gone through the ups and downs then. I have firm boundaries now. I've learned that you cannot do it all on your own—nothing good comes from that. You need to allow others to help you because that's how you grow and that's how your business scales. I have thrived in the last few years by putting trust in others and giving space for error. My business is better for it, and the relationships that I have built as a result are invaluable.

I've learned that relationships can be healing if you let them be. I've learned to be vulnerable to those who have supported me along the way. To burst into random tears and *not* apologize for it. Relationships ebb and flow, and so does the grief. It's human nature to not like change, and grief? Well, it changes you. It will alter every relationship around you. The ones you thought were indestructible now hang by a thread. The ones that were nonexistent suddenly appear and take you by surprise.

At some point I realized that just going with it—allowing change to happen and relinquishing the control—was the only way to get through this. I was holding onto everything so tightly because I couldn't let go of trying to control every situation. If I did, what would happen? Who would emerge? Who would I be? What were people going to see? Were they going to like me? Was I going to like me?

I decided to let go and let things just happen; to just be. To salvage the relationships I had in my life and to pave a way for future ones. And that was when things started happening. I gave in. I gave in to change. I gave in to the grief. I let life happen. I said yes to things. I let people in. I know now that great leaders need great leaders; teams, mentors, clients, and peers—we all need one another. We can do anything, but we can't do everything alone. I learned to start small, to let people know where I was, and to tell people what I need. I know I was definitely surprised when I started to ask for help in small ways, and the most amazing people showed up in my time of need. *They are there, and they are waiting to be asked. Let them in.*

Take small steps to get your life to where it needs to be. If this means getting out of bed in the morning, then amazing job! There was a time when everything felt so big, so hard. I'd wake up with "the should have, could have, would have" mindset. What I say to that now is *go*: go to "shoulds-ville," stay for a little bit but don't pack a bag. It's kind of like going to visit your in-laws: you plan for a short visit. Sit in it, feel it, and then leave it. Frame your day in possibility and gratitude. A little bit each day will go a long way.

For the last seventeen years, I have been processing. The loss of a mother. The pain of what she has missed. The fact that my kids and husband will never get to know what a loving, kind, giving woman she was. Some years it hits harder than others. Looking back now at everything I have accomplished and gotten to experience and become is pretty damn incredible, but it is without her, and that is really hard.

Survivor guilt is a real thing. It's not being able to be truly happy about anything because you always remember that the person you've lost will never be able to celebrate with you or experience life themselves. The work is never-ending, and self-development is key. Giving yourself space when you need it is so important. It's okay to take the time to heal, to breathe, to cry, and to scream. It's okay to fuck off from the world and do what you need to do to survive.

Just know there are people waiting with open arms when you get back, people who want to embrace you and support you on your journey.

If I leave you with anything, it is this:

1. Be empathetic and kind to everyone because you never know what someone is dealing with.

2. Never apologize for being strong-willed; go after your dreams and live life to its fullest.

3. Ask for help, as there are people that want to give it to you. You just need to let them in.

I was nineteen years old when I became a statistic. I became part of a club that I never asked to join when my mother chose to end her life. But it is because of her that I can show up after all of this. No matter how fragile she was at the end of her life, she was still the strongest woman I have ever known.

FIND THE
MAGIC. IT IS
EVERYWHERE.
PULL UP TO
IT, BUY INTO
IT, CATCH THE
STRENGTH OF
ITS BACKDRAFT,
AND START
FLAPPING YOUR
WINGS.

NANCY MACDONALD

NANCY MACDONALD

Nancy Macdonald, owner of an art studio (not just) for children, has had the great privilege, joy, and mess of serving more than 6,600 aspiring artists. After becoming a mother, everything made sense to her, and the art school is a further opportunity to love, nurture, and empower others. Her love of the unexpected, coincidence, hidden meaning, and humor are thrown onto every canvas. Nancy lives to dispel the myth that all artists are starving or are any singular adjective or experience. When she isn't in studio, she is found trying to get her family to play with her outside or listen to her very long stories.

Website: www.artstudioforchildren.com

FB/IG: G @artstudioforchildren @nanceromance.to

My gratitude goes to all those who support and appreciate my work, all my loves who hold me up, believe in me and see me better than I am, and my great and unrelenting teacher, life.

CHAPTER 6

THE BLANK CANVAS

My story trickled out with painstakingly slow speed and the silent deafening hum of a leaky basement faucet. This was the first time in my life that I have ever wished for quick and thorough gossip. The telling for me was a very hard part.

For an intensely private person, there is no hiding from the eventual telling of your separation. Your status changes overnight. A new box to tick, an empty finger, a new prefix. You have no choice but to be public. But I had needed to wait to be strong enough to share my story with those who did not deserve my tears. It was one thing to cry with your best friend but quite another to sob uncontrollably with the neighborhood crossing guard.

Sharing the truth of my failed marriage was the presenting of a whole bouquet of dead flowers. All the promise, beauty, and innocence in that bridal bouquet was now an eerie, foul-smelling assortment of weeds. The flowers are not dead on their own—we forgot to water them, they got sick from us, there was something unbeautiful, unwell about us, and we poisoned it. I loathed its sour smell of failure.

-an excerpt from my blog, My Family Is Not Broken

This is a business story, but it is also a life story. When you are an entrepreneur and a single mom, you cannot help but have all the colors blend. Unlike with paint, when we mixed all the colors together, we did not get brown or mud, we got a beautiful, bold, dynamic experience. It was good to be us. We were proud and capable. It was a different household, but a good one.

Art Studio for Children (ASFC) began as many businesses do, out of a need and a desire. My youngest, who was energetic, emotional, and prone to epic meltdowns, would comfort herself in her room by drawing. One day I was astonished to find her drawing a house with perspective. No one had taught her this technique. I can't remember her age, but I do know while making these "architectural" drawings, she was sucking on a soother (admittedly, this went on a little too late). I realized over time that I had to feed and nurture this talent and passion. We began looking for art classes for her, and there weren't any close by. This wise one turned to me and said, "Momma, you could teach art here." I look back now and realize she handed me my next career and one of the great loves of my life. Solutions and surprises come from unexpected places when you are paying attention.

I held a class for her and one for her older sister each week. It was populated solely by their friends, at our dining room table. The initial motivation, if you remember, was to nurture my children's creativity and artistic side. I did not expect it to grow, and it did, almost in spite of me. Soon, there were more classes and more students. There was no digital marketing in those days (pre-social media), but I benefited tremendously from WOM (word of mom). Where many women want the mess out of their homes, I loved the traffic at my door, the energy coming in, and the idea it was HQ for something special and unique. My children took pride in this, loving that it was happening at theirs. Not long after, we left the dining room table and they allowed me to share space in the basement playroom.

THE PERFECT FAMILY

It was still a very small business at that point in the basement. Looking back, I believe I kept it that way. If that sounds counterintuitive to the entrepreneurial creed, it was because I was in the marathon of my life, and I needed to pace myself. Trying to maneuver a very difficult marriage and keep the innocence and playfulness in my children's lives ate up all my energy. I had no more to give.

On the surface, we looked like the perfect family. Two beautiful, healthy daughters, an enormous community of loving supportive family and friends, an active social life, a home that was ours in a wonderful, treed neighborhood with good schools. We were an attractive couple with all the right stuff. Inside I was dying.

I weighed my life on a balance scale. All the good stuff tipped so high on the right, while the hidden stuff on the left sunk low, hitting the ground with an eerie scraping, metal-against-concrete sound. I chose for a long time to try to see the high side and quiet my sadness and desperation. *Don't be selfish, Nance, think of your children. My children, my family, and my friends would be devastated. Take one for the team. For better or worse.* There were two wolves banging hard on my door. I wrestled the ugly one to the ground daily and let the friendly, loving one in, and fed it. But the ugly one was too hungry, too demanding, too persistent, and it finally broke down the door. It was the day the piano fell on my head. You know the cartoon. No amount of distraction or fooling can save you from accepting the truth because you are flattened by it.

I had begged for clarity. I asked for a sign that I could leave my marriage and got three. The truth is that I had dozens of reasons, but I needed permission. My mom gave me monogrammed towels that Christmas and although I had taken my husband's name, these reflected my maiden name. She could not believe she had made this error. Then I developed an acute case of eczema (I'd never had this condition before, nor have I had it since) on my ring finger and had to take off my wedding rings. And finally, I found something damning hidden under our bedroom dresser. What drew me to look in that very narrow space? My surrender for clarity. That was it. It is important to say it was not three strikes you are out after fifteen years of marriage. It was not hand towels with the wrong name, or a pesky rash, it was the last three straws of a dead marriage. I told my children's father to leave. And he did.

SURRENDER

The next day I got up, raw and exhausted, put on a colorful full pink dress (my mom says when life is going well, wear a nice dress; when life is going badly, wear a nice dress) and took my kids to their first day of school, grades four and seven at the time. In the playground, surrounded by my community, a large wind came up and blew that dress right up over my head. It didn't faze me. I was about to bare more than just my underwear.

But I couldn't just yet. I held my secret close. I did not know how to share this terrible news. I felt like I was breaking hearts. I went through all the motions, faking it to everyone, even my children, and at night, I pushed my face into my pillow and cried. During this time, I had my (very small) business to run, crushing bills, dark sadness, and my children to whom I felt the need to pretend everything was okay. Finally, the very difficult telling allowed people in and lifted a weight. Each reaction was as unique as the next. I was astonished at the depth of love from my village.

The scale on the right now fell so low to the ground. The other scale flew up, filled with possibility, authenticity, and power. They switched. It was a tabula rasa moment, both scary and hopeful. For the first time in my life, I wanted to go to a psychic. She told me two things that stayed with me: you will be fine financially, and you will meet a man by the water. I chose to believe both but to believe more in the power of my choice to believe than any power of a psychic.

During this time of surrender, the truths kept jumping out from behind bushes everywhere I went and in everything I did. It was very hard, but it also demonstrated the magic of letting go to let come. There were so many deep lessons in those early days; life had an ethereal quality.

My basement studio was filled with students and beauty. Every day there was a show of support—flowers, payments for more classes, new students, casseroles, and acts of kindness. My mom painted my bedroom a new color, believing in the power of reframing the place where we start and end each day. My best friend, smart and equipped with an MBA, met with me every Wednesday night to help me strategize. Another looked for a puppy for me. I was being held up by those around me because I was holding myself up. Fortune favors the brave.

MOVING FORWARD

The studio has always been a lab in my life—I go there to escape difficulty and get lost in the doing. I go there to excavate the problems and shine a light on them. I find answers there to big life questions.

The universe I both continued to surrender to and work my ass off for rewarded me. In time, more classes filled, large canvas privates were requested and executed, and art parties and events took off. I approached my children's school to run a program and ended up teaching sixty-five students there every week. It gave me the confidence to approach other schools. Since 2006, ASFC has served more than fifteen schools in the Greater Toronto Area. In fact, at the time of this writing, I am both astounded and proud to have worked with more than 6,600 students.

Original Family Portraits was born of the one I had done for my dad's seventieth birthday gift, which then, hung over the fireplace at our cottage. So many people saw it and wanted one of their own that it became a regular offering. To date, I have done more than 600 of these.

Just before separation, I painted a 40x60" canvas solid and ominous black. Very soon after separation, I added beautiful white daisies. *Daisies at Midnight* represented the power of hope and beauty in adversity. Before this time, I had never used black paint, preferring only color.

I was beginning to understand that the black paint gives the color integrity and value. Joy and pain.

Many of my students could not get enough of weekly classes and those were the children who begged for ART CAMP. This sleepover camp started with one week of camp a summer and grew to be a weekly camp and a large revenue source for me. It was a tremendously dizzying amount of work—I did all the meals, activities, yoga, morning runs, swims, and games, along with very ambitious art projects. In time, it was every week of the summer and often had a waitlist.

I woke each morning those days feeling like a nurturer, a woman, a mom, wanting to make a beautiful house, with good food cooking and all the things in the right place—nice things to wear and eat and surround us, but I also have been the warrior—fearlessly protecting my home, my children, and myself. No matter how hard I worked, how deeply I loved, I was "short a man" on my team. I had a superhero complex, but if I am going to be honest, there were gaps, and I was stretched.

GROWING AND EXPANDING

In 2008 my dear friend Sam called me from Winnipeg, where she had been living with her young family, to tell me she was returning to Toronto; she was separating from her husband of many years. She asked me to find a house close to ours. I looked out my home's back window and across the street where there was a sweet home for sale. She bought that house sight unseen and made her life forty-nine sidewalk squares from us. She and her two daughters became family to us. If I was able to do the impossible in those days, it was because of her.

Having an art school in and out of your home was not always easy. There was a lot of schlepping materials from the home studio to the field and back again. I spent many years in all weather, carrying heavy supplies from school to school to corporation, heavy doors and several flights of stairs, the little people going in the opposite direction on their way to recess, twelve canvasses stacked wet—be careful, tight rules about *when to arrive and you better be packed up and leave before the end of lunch bell.*

For many years, we had only one washroom in our home. Some days ten JK students would arrive in wet boots, snowsuits, hats, and mitts in my very small foyer, I would help them remove their wet items, teach art, and then do the reverse. It had always been important to me that I be at home when my children got back from school. I had this romantic attachment to homemade soup on the stove and me in a studio filled with students when they arrived home. They would pop down, give me a hug, and say hi to the students. This is the way we lived. It was a family affair. We were a three-legged easel, holding each other up, stronger for each other, supporting one another, everyone pitching in. My girls helped with art events, marketing, and even the launch of our wearable art division. In time, we renovated to include a brand-new studio with natural light, ample space, and another bathroom.

There is a theory that if we incorporate what we loved at age ten into our daily adult lives, we will be happy. My art school has always been focused on imagining what I would have loved at that age and—double bonus—in so doing, I have nurtured my ten-year-old self. This happiness for both you/your artist and me is no coincidence, and it has contributed to the success of what I do.

UTILIZING MY SKILLS

My whole life I had wanted to be a writer, but I never had anything to write about. Now, I had a fabulous, delicious buffet of life experiences to share. In 2010 I launched a blog on my birthday. It was my way of narrating my story and not allowing others to do so. As Brené Brown says on her website, "When we deny *our stories*, they define us. When we own *our stories*, we get to write a brave new ending." I know this is true. I had stopped running from the truth, and I was ready to take the poetry of my experience and share it.

My blog was about how hope endures, humor saves us, and moving things forward makes all the difference in the world. That has been my mantra in love, life, and work. In twenty-four hours, it had over 1,000 hits. Within the first week, CBC reached out to book an interview, which I subsequently did. I was invited to be a paid writer as the single parent voice for a popular website. I wove my experiences out in the world and those in the studio into my writing. I had nothing to hide and felt so alive. I was 100 percent myself, and I was so happy. It was a renaissance.

Around the same time, I began to date. This was a further manifestation of my hopefulness, my need to be open to possibility. I wondered about the "man by the water." By a water cooler, puddle, kiddie pool, ocean, in a rainstorm? Drop me a hint, life! Am I warm? At a regatta in 2012, I met a man by the water who proved to be the love of my life. We were married September 2021. Someone recently said, "I love a happy ending." First, nothing over here is done and tied up with a bow, and second, the middle was very happy. I will always count those single-mom days as some of the happiest of my life because I chose to make it so.

In life, in work, and in love—here is my "tool kit twenty."

1. Say yes to life.
2. Find opportunities in new places, stages, and moments.
3. Decide every year that you are in your prime.
4. Pay attention to signals, signs, and coincidences; they are the traffic lights of your life.
5. When profit is down, turn up the customer experience, spend out, and dig in.
6. Choose your community wisely—people are connectors, enablers, cheerleaders, and secret trainers for your best self.
7. Doing what you love works but not without a business mindset and an offer of something people need and want.
8. Always work from a position of abundance—you are enough; you have enough.
9. Find your anthem. This is your power song, your "fake it till you make it" hymn, your "watch out world" aria. Play it when things are great to create the serotonin reflex. Play it when you are down, and voilà—instant lift.
10. Don't convince. You don't need every customer. You don't need that boyfriend.
11. Find the magic. It is everywhere. Pull up to it, buy into it, catch the strength of its backdraft, and start flapping your wings.
12. Life is full of surprises; decide you are too. Never cease to amaze yourself with what you can do.
13. Momentum is powerful. All it takes is one step at a time.

14. If you are not a little embarrassed every year by something you did five years ago, you aren't taking enough risks.

15. New customers are gold. Current customers are platinum. I treat both with gratitude and respect and receive it in return. Every new customer gets a happy dance, the red carpet, and an invitation to meet.

16. Boundaries are critical. Protect that undefended border—your personal life.

17. Stay open, stay (a little) foolish, stay hungry (to paraphrase Steve Jobs).

18. Pivot. Stay fresh. Lean in.

19. Ask for what you want. Politely.

20. Amor Fati. Love your life. Even the hard bits.

When the pandemic hit in March of 2020, I canceled all my in-person programming, as everyone did, and pivoted very quickly to Zoom art with kits. I had never done anything like this before and was absolutely amazed at the results and my ability to articulate steps and guide virtually. I saw an increase in business and an attitude toward the universal importance of a creative experience in the challenge. Now, we have shifted back to in-person classes, the masks are off, and a new chapter at the studio has begun.

Art serves us when we suffer but also serves as an expression of our joy. I always knew this, but the world has finally woken up to it.

My canvas is so beautiful.

I STARTED ASKING WHY NOT ME? WHY CAN'T I HAVE A BUSINESS THAT I LOVE TO SUPPORT MY FAMILY?

MELANIE ZILTENER

MELANIE ZILTENER

Melanie Ziltener is a total word nerd who has been writing since she could hold a pen! Language can change minds and influence others, and Mel loves using that power to support women-led businesses. Otherwise, you can find her reading, gardening, or chasing her five-year-old.

Website: www.tripodcopy.com

FB/IG: www.instagram.com/mel.the.word.nerd

To my grandpa, John McKenzie, who gave me the storytelling gene, and to my son, Wolf, who is keeping the tradition alive.

CHAPTER 7

WHY NOT ME?

Have you ever written down a word and then stared at it for a really long time because even though you know it's spelled correctly, it somehow looks wrong? Now imagine that feeling—that uncertainty and unease—but it's actually your career and your business. That is how I felt. I'm Mel, and I'm a copywriter and content strategist.

Since you may not know me, let me paint a picture using *The Princess Diaries* (because, obviously . . . it is amazing!). I'm Mia at the beginning. We both wear thick glasses, have big eyebrows, and have fallen hard onto bleachers. We are both big dorks, but there are some key differences—I didn't get the makeover from a sassy stylist (although if you know someone, it probably wouldn't be a bad idea). I have glasses and big eyebrows, and while my grandmother is undoubtedly a queen, she's not Julie Andrews. I'm not going to rule a country or have a ridiculous "meet cute" by falling into a fountain.

However, when our stories changed direction, we both fought it. It was difficult for us to come to grips with what that meant and how to move from existing in a role to thriving in another. Simply put—it took me way too long to realize that I could be a princess . . . I mean, emerging content superstar!

BACK TO THE BEGINNING

When my son was born, I knew I wanted to be home with him. If anyone was going to raise him and mess him up, it was going to be me. However, I quickly realized I was not built for it. While he is one of the most extraordinary, funniest human beings on the planet, my brain could not handle the slower pace. I was used to having a million things on the go, and this was killing me. So, I did "the mom things." I tried to start a mommy blog, but that underscored the terrifying realization that I didn't know what I was doing. (Although I did learn that "Just Let Them Play with an Empty Kleenex Box—Enriching Activities for Your Two-Year-Old"-type articles were very easy to write.)

Since my background was in various administrative roles, the next option was to be a virtual assistant. I don't want to brag, but I'm pretty good at it. I'm not spectacular, but I kept things running, gained a couple of great clients, and it was starting to grow. Was it my passion? No. Was it something that paid for diapers and formula? Absolutely. Did it give me a distraction from singing "Twinkle Twinkle Little Star" on repeat? Thankfully, yes. So no, it wasn't fulfilling. *(To any virtual assistants out there, this is in no way a reflection of the work you do, because you and I both know that SO many people would be absolute failures without you! It just didn't light me up!)*

So, I was feeling unfulfilled, but I was also feeling a lot of guilt. Shouldn't I be grateful? I was home with my son, watching him grow in amazing ways, and I was paying the bills. Shouldn't that be enough? I was going through the motions—kind of sleepwalking through my business.

When my son was a baby, it was enough. I was spending enough of my creative energy just figuring out this whole "mom thing." But the older he got, the more natural it became, and I needed something that challenged me. I felt a bit trapped, like the creative part of my brain was pounding at the door, begging for something to do!

Here's what I've learned: weight can be subjective. Imagine stretching out your arm while holding a pen. It's not heavy, is it? What about after an hour? Two hours? A day? A tiny pen can feel a lot heavier than its mere ounces. That's what I felt like. In the grand scheme of things, my personal feelings about my business were not "existential life crisis" sort of heavy. But it felt like a grind, and that sort of gnawing feeling grew. I needed to do something about it. The problem? I didn't know what to do. I wasn't excited, but it was comfortable. Was it worth it to risk something comfortable and secure in hopes of something as intangible as a feeling? And what would I even do? What was I even qualified to do? Plus, I couldn't distance myself from it long enough to even consider what the next steps were. I was too busy doing the job to pay the bills to think if I even wanted to do the job.

Fortunately, this isn't a story about being comfortable or grinding along. This story is about changing direction. Because . . . *record scratch* COVID-19 happened, and I spiraled into a pit of anxiety. Here we were, staring at this unknown disease that had shut down the world.

Everything changed, and I could not change anything about that.

CHANGING DIRECTION

I did what any micromanager would do. I focused on the one thing I had complete control over: my business. I knew I was enjoying writing and had picked up a couple of other small gigs doing it, so I wanted to go in that direction. Plus, like many others, the pandemic gave me the first chance in a long time to examine what I was doing with myself and my life. Since life could change at any time, it felt like the right time for me to change too. Why should I stop at "paying the bills" and instead, go for something bigger? Something more aligned with my actual value?

But I still wasn't committing. When people asked what I was doing, I would downplay it: "I'm doing a bit of freelancing." "Oh, odds and ends." "I'm doing a bit of admin work, a bit of blog writing. It keeps me busy." (In hindsight, those wishy-washy answers make me cringe. They either made me sound like I was a terrible secret agent making up a cover on the spot or a total idiot.)

I figured it would take me a few years to build this up, but something happened that was the catalyst for much faster movement. I had a call with Lianne Kim shortly after joining Mamas & Co. We had a mutual client who had shared that I was doing some writing for her. As we were chitchatting about that, Lianne said, "So you're a content strategist, not really a VA." And I stopped her, saying something along the lines of, "Okay, Lianne, I think that's a little much. We talk about her goals, and I write some stuff that's helping her reach them."

She looked me square in the Zoom eye (which still packs a punch) and said, "No, that is what a content strategist does and that is a skill that people need." When someone confident says something confidently about you, I've learned that you must pay attention. That's what happened—I paid attention, even though I didn't quite believe it. I went along with it, although in my heart, I really was just humoring Lianne. We've heard of impostor syndrome, but this felt more like when my son tells me that he has gone to the moon. Yes, I wanted to write, but being so out there and confident about it felt inconceivable. In fact, that is what had me running two businesses at once. I was so convinced that I would never make it as a content strategist that I was working just as hard at my VA business. If you think it was tough to juggle, you are correct.

But it has taken me a long time because I wanted that security net . . . just in case. It's like I got so used to the weight of doing something I wasn't excited about that it ended up being a lot harder than I thought to let go. And don't get me wrong; I had my support group cheering me on. But the voice in my head was louder and stronger. The voice saying "this will go badly" was there 24/7.

Anyone who has ever had to argue with me on something I'm set on knows I don't go down without a fight. Even I had a hard time arguing with myself, and my negative mindset was very compelling at coming in with a lot of fear. There were a lot of issues I realized were holding me back.

First, I had a guidance counselor who told me that I would never succeed without a university degree. While I now recognize that as a dangerous falsehood (and also, have you coauthored a book, Pamela? That's what I thought!), it was something I didn't realize I was carrying around with me that made me feel like I hadn't earned a seat at the table. Seriously, every time I introduced myself and said, "I'm a content strategist," I expected someone to say, "How dare you?! Where are your qualifications?" As if that's an actual thing that happens in everyday life. (No one said fear was reasonable. . . .)

Second, I had a hard time trusting other women. I was bullied in school in that insidious way that is more cruel glances and less getting pushed into a locker. It's mean and subtle and I kept my guard up. Someone interested in me working with them, someone I imagined to be a "cool kid," surely wasn't *actually* interested. (This must be some sort of elaborate prank.)

Third, failure terrified me. In our family, that is simply not what we do. We work hard and bleed and sweat until it works out. If it's still not working out, it's because we haven't worked, bled, and sweated enough. Failure is not an option, and I certainly did not want to be the one who broke that streak. I knew I wasn't going to fail at being a VA because it was comfortable. I could do it with my eyes shut. But this . . . I wasn't as sure. And I hated that uncertainty.

Finally, success also scared me. I know myself. I know how much I will pour myself into something when I'm passionate about it. Without defining success *very* carefully, I knew I could easily get sucked into a situation where this business would consume me, costing me more time and energy than I wanted it to. That was never a risk being a VA.

All of this came together in a giant ball of feelings, nerves, and stress at every step. Let's be clear: if this is about my entrepreneur journey, then know that it's a journey that didn't go away overnight. It's not like we had a movie moment of me taking a list of my insecurities and throwing them into the ocean, symbolically ridding myself of them for all time. What happened was I kept putting one foot in front of the other. I started asking "what if" in a way that was full of possibility instead of fear. I went into calls and faked my confidence because I wasn't feeling it.

I also started looking at the other people around me. They were setting boundaries, pricing at their worth, and being successful for it. And while they were special and amazing, I realized they did not see me as their inferior. They saw me as a peer. Someone equally worthy of value and respect. I looked at the people ahead of me. They didn't flinch when asking for what they wanted, or what they could do. They just did it.

GAINING CONFIDENCE

So, instead of wondering why me, I started asking why *not* me? Why can't I have a business that I love to support my family? Why can't I take the parts of me that might be weird, unconventional, and a little kooky and use them to my benefit? Because dorky is another word for passionate, and weird is just another word for creative. And I've got that in spades. The more that happened, the more I showed up with actual confidence. I stopped faking it and started kicking butt because I believed I could.

This whole process changed a lot of things—I realized what I could be. I began to reconcile the fact that how I felt and what was true were not always the same thing. However, I realized that I'm more than that. I spent way too much time thinking about what this business meant in terms of who I am when I realized that who I am is a mosaic. There are so many other areas of my life that more fully define who I am and my purpose in life. Even the best-written content in the world doesn't define me the way that my faith, my family, and my service to the community do. Regardless of what title is on my business card, I have a much clearer sense of who I am.

I also learned what happens when I set boundaries. Being in an administration role and then as a VA, I was used to yielding to my bosses and clients. I was supporting them at the expense of myself. The fear of failure pushed me beyond what I should have done. "Can you do this, Mel?" was always met with a hearty, enthusiastic yes, regardless of whether I was exhausted, overworked, or burnt out. However, when I started gaining confidence in myself and what I brought to the table, that began to shift. Yes, I'm still all about serving my clients. But I also recognize what that means. Part of my service is leaning into my expertise and asserting myself when I need to. Part of my service is acknowledging that I cannot do it all, and when I say no to the things that are not my zone of genius, I am doing my clients a favor.

When I started to set boundaries, I saw a grounding reminder of why I started this business. It was to allow me to live my life on my terms. To gain control over the life I want to live. To live in service to others and help someone else realize their awesomeness. Success defined that way has made me a more well-rounded and balanced individual.

Even the most well-meaning people out there have given me advice for what's next for my business, but now that I know who I am and what success means to me, I can confidently assess whether it makes sense for me. As I write this chapter, I think about how I spent my day. Yes, I was busy working, and now I'm typing this late into the evening. But I also got to pick up my son after school. And I spent time with my husband today—actual quality time. We worked together to help out a friend. I'll go to bed tonight satisfied with what I gave today, including the work I did in my business. And I did it all in track pants; I mean, I'm building a really freaking awesome life.

I wish I could say that all my mindset issues are neatly resolved and I'm all like "Impostor, Shmimpostor." But that would be a massive, bald-faced lie. The truth is, even the kick-off meeting to write this book felt like I was playing on the kids' team in an NHL game. Being in the same sentence as these women feels surreal and it was a little terrifying to write something that would be held up next to them.

But here's what I can tell you. When those moments happen, I am better equipped to handle them. I can pause, ask myself if that sounds realistic and value myself enough to know that I deserve to be able to set and uphold boundaries. Yes, it's a work in progress, but it's *progressing*. It would never have happened this way if I kept playing small and afraid. It would never have happened this way if I wasn't committed to being uncomfortable, learning, and taking it one day at a time. It would never have happened if I wasn't ready to let go of something that felt comfortable and set boundaries to build something that protects the life that I love.

Here's the thing: If I had done nothing, I would have been okay. But I would have still been doing the grind and carrying that same old weight. Why should the bar only be okay?

I may not have had those moments, those small growth moments that brought on big changes. I wouldn't have been helping others and serving others in the best way that I could. I wouldn't wake up and do something that I love. I wouldn't feel lighter as I start each day. Maybe I would have been okay. But settling for less than what could be . . . *that* is not okay.

Now, I see how I'm making an actual difference for my clients in a way that honors the best parts of me. They're getting in front of more people and getting the attention that they deserve. In sales calls and podcasts, they're flexing their authority because they can reference the content I helped create. They're doing big things in their businesses because they have the headspace to do it! I've had the privilege of working with some true powerhouses who are out there making a difference, and I get to be a part of that. It's quite literally a dream come true.

So, my reader, if you are living in fear and mumbling a halfhearted answer when people ask what you do, I want you to know that I get what you're serving up. Instead, try asking yourself, "Why not me?" Try going down the waterslide and see where it takes you.

LEARNING AND GROWING. ABUNDANTLY. WITHOUT LIMIT, WITHOUT RESERVATION. WITH TRUST IN MYSELF, BELIEF IN MY ABILITIES, HOPE, PREPARATION, AND COFFEE. BUT IT DIDN'T START THERE.

ADRIENNE SHNIER

ADRIENNE SHNIER

Adrienne Shnier, MA, PhD, JD, is a mother and founder of two companies. Adrienne is CEO and Advancement Coach & Strategist of Apply Yourself: The Advancement Spot Inc., where she holistically, healthily, and strategically works collaboratively with university students and their families to achieve lives beyond their wildest dreams, often starting with graduate and professional school applications. Adrienne also founded Shnier Mackenzie Law & Policy Consulting, Professional Corporation, serving small businesses, health-related clinics and practices, and regulated and unregulated health professional associations. Adrienne is a professor of health and pharmaceutical policy, regulation, and law at a Toronto university and law school. Adrienne loves kayaking up north or sipping a latte on a nice patio . . . while thinking about what's next!

Website: www.applyyourselfglobal.com

FB/IG: @ApplyYourselfGlobal

I would not be here without the support of my family, and most importantly, my daughter, my husband, and my mother. This is for them, and for you, on your personal and professional advancement journey.

CHAPTER 8

APPLY YOURSELF: ADVANCING FROM SCARCITY TO ABUNDANCE

Learning and growing. Abundantly. Without limit, without reservation. With trust in myself, belief in my abilities, hope, preparation, and coffee. These are themes that have woven themselves throughout my journey through academia and as the CEO of two companies. But it didn't start there.

I grew up around strong women who owned businesses and practices in the health sector. I saw the ups and the downs. I saw the wins and the losses, the 30+ and 50+ year client loyalty, the dedication to serve, the grateful . . . and the ungrateful. The freedom, the ability to choose, the potential, the life beyond business—the kind of life that only running your own business could provide.

My mom was one of these business owners. I often heard stories of how once I was born, she took a two-week mat leave and then brought me to the office with her. Her office was my third home growing up (the second being my grandparents' house, three blocks away from our home. My grandparents ran their own busy medical practice for almost sixty years). My mom, a dentist, ran her own dental practice, fully staffed with supportive, loyal, hardworking, dedicated women, and I saw her passion, her drive, her dedication, and her ability to do what needed to be done. And on top of that, she made it look easy! She took, and still takes, Fridays off. She was at every class trip and every pizza lunch, and she always stuffed Friday folders for my (and my three siblings') elementary school classes. My parents were at every dance lesson (even though I wasn't very good—there is video evidence that my siblings use as blackmail), every gymnastics class, every music class, every everything. And to this day, I don't think I've ever heard the words "I'm tired" from my mom.

My parents discussed business at home, not hiding the challenges and troubleshooting from us. Running a business seemed natural to me. I remember as a teen and young adult driving up and down Toronto streets, naturally imagining what my storefront would look like. I remember a law firm with a relatively boring exterior that I thought had so much potential. These storefronts lived in my mind, rent-free. So, how would I get there? I had absolutely no idea. But that didn't bother me. I generally didn't think about it until about 2020, some years later . . . and here's why.

EARLY YEARS

I wanted to be a doctor . . . or so I thought. I was surrounded by health professionals and assumed that would be my path, too. I entered a highly competitive undergraduate life sciences program at a reputable university in Toronto, where in any given class, I had 2,000 to 3,000 classmates. I took the typical first-year classes—biology, chemistry, physics, calculus, and more, but I struggled. I understood the material, but it *really* didn't interest me. The examination style didn't test my understanding; rather, it tested my memorization skills. I found myself daydreaming through the course calendar, skipping to the global health and public health courses, thinking to myself, *look at how much fun those courses look.* But I had no idea I could have chosen any other program.

Throughout my first year, I witnessed competition-based, scarcity-informed behavior that formed my perspectives on student success. In a chemistry lab, my fumehood partner ruined my test results by filling my test tubes with hydrochloric acid. Looking back, I can see now that she felt so competitive with me and had such a toxic and competitive mindset that it caused her to act out, materially affecting my work. Throughout that formative year, I witnessed other forms of competition-informed behavior—important pages visibly torn from library textbooks (before textbooks were available online through university libraries), shared notes with intentionally wrong information, questions asked in study groups and intentionally wrong answers offered, among others. While the latter wasn't directed at me, the cumulative effects of these behaviors stuck with me. I knew it didn't have to be this way.

In large part because of the environment at this university, I transferred to my now alma mater for the rest of my undergrad journey. I had missed the deadline for entering the biology program, and so I reluctantly entered a social-science-based health policy and politics program—which I ended up absolutely loving. In this program, I met great friends and faculty who changed my life. One faculty member, in particular, taught me the importance of mentorship and the significance of supportive and encouraging professors who were true teachers in every sense of the word—teachers of skills, ways of thinking, critical thought, collaboration, communication, and advocacy. Over the next three years with this professor, who was a feminist (of the 1960s movement) and medical anthropologist, we conducted research deep into the pharmaceutical industry, conflicts of interest, regulation, marketing, and fraud. I was totally hooked.

Based on our research, and with this same professor as my adviser throughout graduate school, I completed my Master's and PhD, then my law degree. I had the best time with the most supportive committees in graduate school and finished my PhD in just shy of four years. In 2015 I had been working on my dissertation in Starbucks, which garnered the attention of university students (and their parents) who were applying to graduate and professional schools, including Master's, PhD, medical, law, and other programs. They would ask if I would review their applications and, quickly, fellow coffee-sippers would know my routine and would come to Starbucks with their materials for my help. Incredibly, this was the beginning of my company, *Apply Yourself: The Advancement Spot Inc.*, which began based on my experience with, and my client's success in, receiving offers of admission to graduate and professional programs at Ivy League schools internationally.

CAREER LIFE

Formatively, after my PhD, I immediately became a professor of health policy, pharmaceutical policy and regulation at a Toronto university, while I went to law school as a student in the next building. Again, I found myself in a hypercompetitive environment where I witnessed extremely toxic and unhealthy vices, habits, and behaviors owing to stress, overwhelm, and competition among peers. This time, I felt much more secure with more trust in myself, and my abilities, and I had additional perspective as a professor. I saw everything from prescription-sharing to alcohol use in the mornings, to illicit drug abuse to attempt to deal with stress. This was undeniably distressing to me—a drug policy researcher and current professor seeing the effects of socially constructed competition unraveling around me in real time. I vowed to do something about it, and thankfully, *Apply Yourself* became the vector for this change.

In 2019 I graduated from law school, passed my bar exams, and began articling at a respected, established litigation firm in downtown Toronto. Up until this point, I worked like a horse, finishing four degrees in twelve years. It didn't matter if it was an evening, weekend, or vacation. If I was there, so was my laptop. A few months into articling, my husband and I decided to start a family—a radical shift from my career-centric focus. In fall 2019, I was happily pregnant. My "plan" was to quickly and seamlessly give birth and promptly start working at a litigation firm downtown with aspirations of one day opening a firm. In March 2020, I was interviewing at firms downtown and was offered positions at these firms. Then COVID hit.

I remember standing in my articling firm's foyer with the staff watching the news from the TV on the wall as, one by one, societal institutions and social services shut down. We all went home that day and remote working began. My university teaching shifted online. Wearing masks to protect oneself and others from the spread of germs went from being "discriminatory" to being legislated. I was seven months pregnant. We were in lockdown. No family, no friends, no gym. My job offers dissolved as the uncertainty set in. Months earlier, my husband and I had hired a doula to support us in the hospital (my lawyer side wanted another educated set of eyes on the delivery). Slowly, hospital policies began to tighten as well, prohibiting support people from attending to labor and delivery. Later, "bubbling"—isolating with a small group of people—became a thing. So, we "bubbled" with my family, our primary support over the pandemic.

My call-to-the-bar was a "paper call," meaning that what would have otherwise been a wonderful ceremony at a beautiful venue surrounded by friends and family was a purely administrative and completely underwhelming activity. It was still special for me, however, because my paper call-to-the-bar was scheduled for my due date, and my husband, who is also a lawyer, administered my Oath and signed my paperwork in our upstairs home office, which later became our daughter's room.

OUR BIRTHING JOURNEY

I was eight days past my due date, so an induction was scheduled for a Wednesday at 3:30 p.m. At this time, in June 2020, the hospital policy was that one single support person could attend. My parents drove me, and my mom came in with me because my husband continued to work in the office. I changed into the gown and was ready for the procedure when we were hastily informed that my mom had to leave immediately because my husband was attending the labor and delivery the next day and the support person had to be the same on both days. My parents waited for me and drove me home. I was feeling nervous, isolated, and uncomfortable only at the beginning of a long process that was completely foreign to me. My lawyer brain was firing on all cylinders, imagining all the horrible things that could happen with no one around. I had recently been working on labor negligence cases where otherwise healthy deliveries went wrong in the worst possible ways. I was terrified and having nightmares, worried that a doctor or nurse would miss something, that the reduced staffing would result in something going terribly wrong, and that no one would be there to help me or advocate for me.

The next stage of induction was at 8:30 a.m. with only my husband (I love him, but he's no doula, and he certainly isn't my mother, who I knew would medically advocate for me if needed). The next morning, the induction continued, and five hours later, my water still hadn't broken. The on-call OB tried over a period of about two to three hours to break my water.

Eventually, it broke, and the induction medication really kicked in. It all came on full force—my own contractions on top of the medically induced contractions. Though our doula helped us over the phone, she wasn't there, but we got the peanut labor ball, so that was a win. Over a period of about two hours, I went from handling the contractions well to not being able to breathe because of the overlapped contractions. I was in immense pain, in tears, and gasping for breath. My husband called our doula for help, and she was the first person to suggest an epidural that day. I could no longer speak or catch a breath. It was time for the epidural. Just in time, we made the request for the only anesthesiologist before he went to perform a C-section.

I got the epidural and then my temperature spiked. Of course, I knew that increased temperature was a common side effect of epidurals, but at that moment, the medical team decided to start taking my temperature because of new COVID protocols. One minute my temperature was a cool 36.9, and the next it was 37.4. The nurse told me I was now "presumptive positive." I told her we had been fully isolating since March (it was now June), and I had just had the epidural. She went to check the new hospital policy and said that 37.4 was the low end of the "presumptive positive" threshold, but she would check with her nurse manager to see if the fact that I had an epidural would change anything. Five minutes later, she returned and said that we were in luck because the *new* threshold was 37.5. I ripped off the covers and my husband stealthily ran to get ice to lower my body temperature before my next temperature check. It worked: down to 37.2. Phew. Then I fell asleep, and my temperature went up to 37.5. Darn. "Presumptive positive." Suddenly the OB and nurses had to gown and de-gown every time they entered my delivery room. The only perk was that I got a private (isolation) recovery room without having to pay out-of-pocket for it. Score.

I was able to "relax" for about three hours and then it was go-time. The room went from peaceful and dark to stadium-lit like I was about to perform for 50,000 people. Fifteen minutes later, our daughter was born at 1:04 a.m. Lights dimmed.

All I cared about at that point was prolonged cord cutting and skin-to-skin contact, so that's what I advocated for and that's what happened. My husband had five minutes to hold our newborn before he was swiftly booted out. Quick picture, and he was gone. I held our daughter on my chest while my husband was ushered one way down the hall and I was wheeled down the other in my bed. Right turn, left turn, all the walls looked the same. I had no idea where we had been wheeled to. No way to tell anyone where I was, but it didn't matter anyway since no one was allowed to visit, my husband was gone, and I was still very frozen and couldn't walk. And I wasn't allowed out of my isolation room, prohibited from opening the door. I'm not sure which committee adopted the policy that the food for "presumptive positive" new mothers should be left on a tray on the floor on the opposite side of the closed door. Luckily, one of our friends had warned me to pack my own nourishing foods because attention during recovery can be less than ideal. As it turned out, even less so in "presumptive positive" isolation.

There I was, alone with my newborn, still terrified that something horrible would happen without anyone there. It was now 4 a.m. My baby did not leave my chest. I was afraid that if I fell asleep, she would be taken for a test (or something) without my knowledge. So, no sleep, no support, no service. Because I was "presumptive positive," the nurses were afraid to enter my room too often, so the only person that came in that morning was an OB to complete an exam on me. That OB taught me how to change a diaper.

Over the next fifteen or so hours, I video-called my husband, my family, and a few of our close friends. I took pictures. I stared in awe at our new baby. In absolute love. Nothing else mattered. I did everything I could to be discharged at the twenty-four-hour mark. I was worried that the shift change overnight would cause a delay. I needed to get out of isolation and get home. I was finally discharged at 3:55 a.m. I called my husband who, while I was in isolation, had slept, gone for a jog, and eaten good food. Okay, time to come get us.

My husband picked up my mom at 4:00 a.m., and they both came to pick us up. In a province-wide lockdown, I wore a mask, but I was terrified of the air that my baby was about to breathe outside of our hospital room. I held a mask over her nose and mouth, and we were quickly wheeled out to the curb—no checking our car seat, not even a goodbye. Then, of course, we couldn't figure out how to tighten the bucket straps, so at 4:30 a.m., I was standing outside with my sleeping baby, in sheer shock and adrenaline-fueled from the last forty hours, while my mom and husband YouTubed the high-tech bucket straps. But I was outside holding my baby, in the fresh air, so I didn't care. Sore, bloated, standing at the exit, waiting to get into the car. Relieved that we made it out of the hospital, that we were no longer "patients" on an institutional clock, and that we were able to just *be*. Able to breathe our own air. Car seat figured out, we dropped my mom off at her house three blocks away from ours and were home by 5:00 a.m. For the first time, my husband really held our daughter, and I had a shower.

For three days my husband was home, but he returned to the office since lawyers were considered to be an essential service. My mom was the only other person to come over, and she came over about every other day for months and months. I was still university teaching without a mat leave, so when my mom visited, I lectured and graded papers. Then, when my husband came home at around 8:00 p.m., I would make dinner, do some more grading and research, nurse our baby to sleep, then work until about 4:00 a.m. This was our schedule for sixteen months.

SHIFTING PRIORITIES

A few months went by, and after understanding what it was to have a newborn and a family, after processing a traumatic birth experience, my priorities shifted. I quickly began to realize that my prior "plan" to return to a law firm after having a newborn was not only unrealistic, but it was also no longer what I wanted. I wanted something different. Everything had changed. I was able to hug my baby all day every day and night for months—sixteen months to be exact. We were able to get into a family rhythm, and without pressure, we chose to bedshare for bonding, nursing, and peaceful sleep. I was able to do research into the different newborn cries—there are seven by the way—so I could learn what they meant and what my baby was trying to communicate. I was able to teach my baby sign language so that she could communicate if she wanted "milk," then later, "more," "water," "food," "all done," and the washroom signs, among others, which made for significantly less crying and significantly more free and curious play, plus she was fully daytime toilet-trained by the time she was one year old. I understood, but realized from experience, that we were raising a little human, not a baby. I was able to lay the foundations for the type of mother I wanted to be with the support of my husband and mother. Even though the pandemic months have been some of the most challenging, I am eternally grateful for the time to grow into myself, into the mother that I have become.

APPLY YOURSELF

Apply Yourself had been a side hustle for half a decade, but once I had my daughter, everything changed. I realized that I had been playing small and that *Apply Yourself* was truly changing the lives of my clients and their families. Parents and their (adult) kids were enjoying each other again because not only was the stress of academic and professional advancement removed from parents, but my clients were also excelling, achieving, and surpassing their goals with my experienced help, structure, and strategies. I realized that I would have to put myself out there publicly, on social media and other fora, which I dreaded. But I couldn't let my fear—of being judged, of other people's opinions—hold me back. If not now, when? And so I started showing up and growing *Apply Yourself* to help as many students and families as I could.

Apply Yourself revolutionizes the university student experience during some of the most intensive times in their lives—throughout their higher-learning experiences, into their professional careers, and beyond. We have a zero-tolerance policy for any competitive-natured or scarcity-based actions, and we happily coach our clients through intense, hypercompetitive graduate and professional school application processes, programs, and environments, reformulating and reconceptualizing academic and professional advancement and success using health-focused practical, actionable strategies. I have served and continue to serve as an Admissions Committee Member and job search / promotion / tenure committee member and have critically reviewed thousands of applications and advocated for amazing, genuine, deserving candidates. From these experiences, I have identified trends and characteristics in the nuances, framing, and communication styles required in successful applications.

Application writing is truly an art. We coach and strategize with our clients on their graduate and professional school applications in my twelve-week course that, quite literally, takes our clients through their graduate and professional school applications—and they become part of our amazing, supportive, encouraging Community in the process. We focus on the individual and their success, *not* "the competition" and "the stats" (we know they exist, but our focusing on them doesn't help us progress constructively in the immediate or long term). We do not feed into what many students are (and I was) exposed to as the narrative of success as being dependent on lack of sleep and unhealthy or toxic vices and habits. The Apply Yourself Community, including in our group and individual programs, as well as our monthly membership, offers continued structure, strategy, support, and accountability for our clients as they determine, work toward, achieve, and exceed their goals, continually advancing and elevating their goals through our work together. Our clients are building lives *beyond* their wildest dreams, and we are so proud to join them on their journeys.

OPENING MY FIRM

Over the course of summer 2020, I decided I would open my own firm. I had the skill, the willingness to learn, trust in my ability, and the motivation for time- and choice-freedom to build the kind of life I wanted for myself and my family. That summer, I built my firm's foundations and set up all my systems. In September 2020, I officially began to serve my dream clients at Shnier Law & Policy Consulting. I practice business and health law, serving loyal women-owned businesses as "external general counsel" for their business growth, strategy, and contract needs over time. I also serve health-related businesses, practices, and regulated and unregulated professional associations. And we're growing—my husband has joined me as a partner and our firm is now called *Shnier Mackenzie Law & Policy Consulting.* I'm loving every minute of it.

In April 2021, my husband, daughter, and I went on one of our usual walks in Toronto, but this walk was different. Something clicked and I decided to look for office space. I'm a fan of making big decisions before I'm officially ready, but just in time for important growth—clear indications of trust in myself, belief in my ability, and hope for the future. And two weeks later, on May 1, 2021, I had possession of my current office space. I spent six months directing construction and built a structure I felt good in and that would work for both *Shnier Law* and *Apply Yourself.*

Today, *Apply Yourself: The Advancement Spot* has grown to be *the spot* for not only graduate and professional school applications but also holistic, healthy, client-focused, customized, support, strategy, and skills development, allowing university students to create and realize incredible lives without thinking about "the competition." The scarcity mindset breeds competitive behavior that has the potential to harm ourselves and others. I've been on the receiving end of that. I am changing the university student experience by focusing on what matters and what is not provided to students—an abundance mindset, personal and professional growth, and application skills that, together, help them to advance and build their lives.

I also host *The Advancement Spot Podcast,* which helps university students and young professionals in their academic and professional success, develop abundance rather than scarcity mindsets, and think big about their futures—kicking fear to the curb. Applications are not just about "getting in": they're about *the lives we create*. And our community is full of supportive, like-minded university and mature students and their families.

Both of my companies are growing. I serve my dream clients. My time is my own. I have learned to trust myself, believe in myself, and have hope for the future. And I am grateful for my abilities. It didn't begin that way, but through intense self-discovery through my experiences, I have learned and grown, and I'm not done yet. I have learned to "apply myself," live, and make decisions from a place of abundance and opportunity, rather than scarcity and competition. I have built businesses that provide me with choice, flexibility, and opportunity—and which allow me to serve and have an important, productive, and constructive impact on my clients' lives. I choose when I work and how I work. I am the mother I want to be—I continue to build my companies with that goal as my priority. And I can't wait to see what happens next.

I THINK I'M
DONE BEING
NICE. FORGET
AVERAGE. I
WANT THE
BUSINESS AND
LIFE OF MY
DREAMS.

CHERNELL BARTHOLOMEW

CHERNELL BARTHOLOMEW

Chernell Bartholomew is a mom to three beautiful girls and a wife to a loving husband. Additionally, she is a Certified Health Coach, A Ritz-Carlton Award-winning Registered Massage Therapist, and a personal trainer. With more than fifteen years' experience in health and wellness, her passion is to help exhausted moms decrease burn-out and stress so they can create vibrant energy and tap into their true needs and desires. She believes that every mom can build that beautiful, healthy life when they put themselves first without deprivation or extremes, all while eating the damn cake. Mindset and obstacles are just part of the transformational process she walks her clients through.

Website: www.vitalitymvmt.com

FB/IG: www.instagram.com/chernell.energycoach

Dedicated to my mom, my daughters, and the woman who always felt average but knows there is something extraordinary inside of her.

CHAPTER 9

SEEN BUT NOT HEARD

I always knew I wanted to have kids, and my becoming a mother has been one of the most awakening experiences of my life: our kids are mirrors of who we are and how we feel. I deeply want them to know they are loved and can be whoever they want to be. And building a business was something I didn't even know I wanted until I realized that I didn't want the standard full-time hustle for myself and my family. I wanted to drop off my kids at school and pick them up. I wanted to be the soccer mom, but I knew I needed a business that would fill my cup and build up other women like me.

FEELING BROKEN

After gaining more than seventy pounds with my first daughter, I felt disconnected from my body. Plus, I was overwhelmed by this new life, putting everyone's needs before my own, and living out of my mom's house and my in-laws' house for over a year until we bought our house. Because of the back-and-forth and eating just to eat whatever was convenient, I wasn't moving my body in the ways I used to. I was experiencing mood swings, forgetfulness, and impatience, I was on edge by the end of the day, and I honestly just expected to be exhausted forever.

Everything I'd seen about motherhood was about giving up your life, and I did that. It didn't work. It broke me. I remember standing in front of the fridge, nine months postpartum, just searching for something to make me feel better. I wasn't even hungry. I remember having a pointless argument with my husband, and I just didn't feel happy. I felt lost. I cried often, until one day I just said no, this has got to change. It was a split-second decision, and at that moment, I knew I wanted to show up differently for my daughter, for my partner, and mostly for myself!

I found an exercise bootcamp close by and booked a trainer on a weekly basis. I needed to book someone so I wouldn't find an excuse to slip back into the background. I needed that accountability because I couldn't do it on my own. Or could I? This thought stayed with me as the months went by.

As I said, I always knew I wanted a family and kids, but I didn't always know I wanted a business. Building my business was different because it wasn't about being busy or following a trainer's directions, and it wasn't about working for praise from a manager or coworker. It was about me feeling like enough. Was I smart enough, capable enough? It was about me not needing anyone else's validation; it was about me deciding that I was a leader and doing it for myself. But I wasn't an expert—I was just me, an average mom.

I was just the daughter of my mom and dad who came to Canada from the beautiful islands of Trinidad and Tobago. They worked hard with full-time (and often part-time) gigs. My mom is a short woman with quiet strength and a giving heart, and my dad is tall with a fighter's mentality. I was taught "people like us" have to work twice as hard to be successful. I'm a first-generation Trinidadian Canadian and the little sister to my older twin brothers. Our family worked hard and trained hard. We've always loved sports, especially track and field. My brothers were top athletes and still had records on the walls when I reached high school. Some of the teachers referred to me as "the twins' sister." Because of the age gap between my brothers and me, I had the best of both worlds. I had annoying big brothers to play fight with and who were my protectors, who took me places, and who bought me stuff. I also had a lot of time alone when I retreated inward or watched Oprah.

Oprah was one of the few black women I saw at the top of her league. Not an actress or athlete. A curvy woman who was confident and showed up in front of all of us every day and asked great questions and transformed lives. As a young woman, I was short and curvy, I didn't look like most of my friends, and I didn't see anyone who looked like me leading industries. I spent most of my time blending in because standing out was scary.

STANDARDS

I have a vivid memory of bouncing through my front door after school and into my kitchen with a test paper in my hand, excited to show my mark to my parents. I put it up on the fridge, and I proudly beamed about how hard I had studied. I felt such accomplishment. I felt smart;

I felt I could really do anything I put my mind to. My mother saw it first, and she cheered me on, smiling from ear to ear, congratulating me. I waited for my dad to get home. He was just in the door, shoes off, and I told him I had some news and pointed to my test paper. He looked at the paper, with a star and a red circle around 95 percent. Almost perfect. He nodded, looked at me, then asked, "So what happened to the other five percent?" At that moment, I crumbled. I realized "almost perfect" wasn't ever going to be good enough.

I would never be the smartest in the room, but I was taught to be polite and respectful. I was taught ladies must be seen and not heard, and that's who I was. I was likable, not outspoken, athletic, but not quite the super athlete. I was the nice girl who got good grades, but I was not a straight-A student. I was all-around good, but I was not very memorable.

I've made several New Year's resolutions as I've grown up to become a stronger woman. I am a recovering people pleaser, and it started long, long ago. It might have even started on that very day.

SELF-DOUBT

My parents separated at the end of my high school career. It was for the best for us all and something we had expected years before. The house had gotten uncomfortable; we were all living our lives and trying not to cross paths too often. Over the years, as a girl and young woman, I got used to shoving down my feelings at home because in the moments I was outspoken or assertive, I was being disrespectful. I stopped testing my voice, not only at home but also at school and in life in general. I avoided making anyone feel bad, I avoided the awkward discomfort that usually followed afterward, and I avoided the feeling of someone not liking me.

I met my husband online when I was seventeen (he is my husband according to us and our taxes). We like to say we started online dating before it was a thing. I would've never told my parents that: to them, and especially to my overprotective brothers, he was a friend of a friend. I was not just the nice girl with him; I was not just someone in the background. I wasn't just "good enough." I felt like I was his dream girl, and he told me that all the time. He was (and is) my dream guy, but I didn't really tell him that often. I've started telling him more. This was more than twenty years ago now, and we used to get stared at when we walked hand in hand, maybe because of our ages, maybe because of our racial differences, or maybe because when we walked together, we both felt proud and confident.

He had a loud and expressive family, and they welcomed me in. I had a hard time with such outward expression of all emotions. Showing negative emotions or being outspoken wasn't for nice girls, right? I found it both exhausting and enlightening to know that families were so open, so outspoken, so willing to say their opinions even if others didn't like it, then sit down to eat dinner with everything returning to normal. I never really had that. Was this normal, or was I normal? We struggled at times to communicate because as much as I love to talk when the good energy is flowing, when I'm experiencing difficult emotions, I shut down—it's like my brain freezes—and I go deeply inward. I become mute, and I block everything out. To my husband, that is the worst thing because he is used to words, explanations, and logic. We've built a family and a life together, we've been through the standard ups and downs, and we are still building this beautiful life our way, despite what tradition says. Kid, house, more kids, and a wedding TBD. Maybe we did it backward, or maybe we did it the way we wanted, because it didn't matter if anyone liked it but us.

My husband grew up in a family where being an entrepreneur seemed to come naturally. The risk involved and the grit to always bet on one-self is his zone of genius. Maybe his confidence rubbed off on me, or maybe I had it all along and finally started giving myself permission to think that way.

After high school, I struggled to find my path. I wanted to use my hands, my knowledge, my actual body, and my energy to help heal people, help them live pain-free, ease stress, give them a safe space to relax and open up, and make them feel pampered and taken care of. Maybe I wanted to give that so much because I felt I needed that safe space too. When I finally made the decision to become a Registered Massage Therapist, it felt so right. I was excited, but I was reminded that massage therapists don't make a lot of money and money was the only way to be happy in a country like Canada, or so I had always heard. I should've decided to become a physiotherapist instead: they make more money, and people respect them more. They have a university degree.

Self-doubt bloomed again: *I don't have a university degree; does that mean I'll make less money? Does that mean I can't find happiness?* We had a magnet on our refrigerator that read "Money is the root of all evil." I read that every day and decided I didn't need to make a lot of money because I was a good person. So, I dove headfirst into massage therapy. My love of human sciences, anatomy, and physiology became deeper every day. I missed the honor roll by a few percentage points. Looking back, I know why. As I write this chapter, the amount of clarity I'm receiving is hitting me in the face, but it is also creating a buzz and a heightened awareness of why I doubt myself and procrastinate.

As a massage therapist, I dreamed about working at high-end spas. I wanted that, but I was supposed to be happy helping people no matter where I worked. The ambiance of the spa, the level of service, the energy of rest and healing, and the quality of clientele—I wanted that. My first spa was in the largest hotel in the city. I loved our team, and my learning how to work with different requests, learning about quotas, balancing life and work, being able to see the systems and backend, learning how to manage different personalities, and being evaluated all helped me create the love I had for working in a spa. During this time, I also became a personal trainer. Another certification; another distinction: maybe I'd be good enough now?

I've always loved movement and have a passion for helping and teaching, and for a few years, I also helped a trainer run his bootcamp. I learned so much there. I discovered my love for kickboxing, which is not surprising because feeling strong and capable is a need for me. I made friends, pushed my body, lifted some heavy shit, and was praised for being not just good but great at something. I became part of a team.

At the same time, I was growing my mobile massage therapy and fitness business. I thought we were growing and expanding and flourishing, and I finally felt in a groove until I was called into the office one day. Because my mobile business was growing, and because the trainer's clients loved working with me, I soon had to choose between a dream and a life I was just starting to create, all to avoid a conflict of interest. On one hand, I was praised for being ambitious, and on the other hand, I was told I had to choose. It felt like a kick in the gut. Again, I was good but not good at the same time. I was too much, and it came with consequences: choose between a dream and life I was just starting to actualize or being a part of a team that helped me realize I had this dream. Choose between me or them. I was falling into that deep silence again. I had hard emotions, and I felt mute and disengaged. I took a deep breath, stuttered, then chose myself. I chose me. I cried some sad tears and some triumphant ones for this choice.

MOVING ON / LESSONS AND REALIZATIONS

Another lesson. Learning to cut ties when they need to be cut instead of holding on and getting burned more in the process. I always say when you run into a brick wall a few times, you realize the only way to not get hurt is to not get close.

I have a hard time keeping promises and deadlines for myself, but if a friend, client, manager, or coach asks me to, I do not hesitate. I am your cheerleader, supporter, and sidekick, but I am not the showstopper. I am the one you can depend on but not the one who sees her ideas to the end.

After working at other hotel spas, I found what I thought would be my forever home as an RMT at one of the highest-rated hotel spas in the city. I was in the 1 percent of RMTs in the city with this position, and it held some weight and credibility. I was making more money and loving the atmosphere. The team, management, and operations were next level. I was among the experts, and I won an award as well. These ladies and gentlemen made me up my game, and I am forever grateful for the friendships I still have.

I started looking for resources, programs, and courses to learn about becoming a coach because I realized a gap in my ability to help my clients. I was restricted within massage therapy; I wanted to help in a more lasting way. I also needed to see other women and moms creating businesses because in my mind, it was impossible. I found an amazing community, and it helped me see that it was possible—it would be messy and sometimes really hard, but it was possible. I was invited on a trip that changed my entire mindset. I didn't think I should've been on a trip with these powerhouse women. They all had amazing businesses that blew me away. I was just me. That week, something changed. I was amazed to have experiences I never even imagined and to hear we were all struggling with similar things but at different levels. I had these ladies on a pedestal, but they were like me in many ways.

I love working specifically with moms experiencing exhaustion and burnout because I was one. At the beginning of my career as a coach, I wanted to help everyone with everything, because I'm nice and I want to save everybody. But looking back at my journey in motherhood made me realize I needed someone not just to say that I was doing a great job but to tell me to take time for myself and actually make me do it. I needed someone to see me going inward and help me sit in the light, to help me realize that I can only give from the overflow of my own cup. Working on myself first without guilt helped me realize that you don't have to disappear into motherhood. This new body was magnificent and deserved to be nourished. The diet culture that had us in a chokehold has no place here, and the energy you put into yourself will create more energy you can use for the people and passions closest to your heart. We are allowed to be playful and passionate and create beautiful lives our way. But everything I saw about coaching said I shouldn't be here. I wasn't a tall white female with two kids, a dog, and a degree in my pocket. I should drink coffee and alcohol a little too much and watch all the latest shows.

The women I have seen in my life who stood up, talked out, and were thought leaders were all super athletes or celebrities. They made lots of money and got lots of love, but they also received a lot of hate. I didn't want lots of money, I didn't want to be known, I didn't want to be labeled arrogant or bitchy. Right? I'm supposed to be unassuming, nice, and compliant. Seen but not heard.

But maybe I'm here for me and you. For my partner and kids and family and for women who grew up just like me. I'm learning there is duality in life. There's this need to make things black or white, either/or, but all my energy resonates with the feeling that this is about both and more. Not being everything to everyone but instead being what I need to be at different stages in my life. Maybe the voice of that little girl trying to just be good enough is getting quieter. Maybe having three daughters, one of whom was born during a pandemic, made me realize that I need to be the one who calls people, places, and energies into and out of my life. Maybe I didn't choose to be a coach or to have a business, but they chose me. They chose me so I can be that safe space, to be the voice that drowns out all the ones that tell you that you're not doing it the right way. I wonder if I had been seen *and* heard, would those people be proud of me? You know what, it doesn't even matter because I am proud of myself. I no longer need anyone else's validation, and it feels wild! Freeing! And scary as hell.

I can be polite and respectful but also assertive, powerful, and confident. I can be a voice for moms in this culture that glorifies exhaustion and deprivation. I help women be heard, and I help them create the health and life they want on their terms so they can lift the heavy shit of life. I think I'm done being nice. Forget average. I want the business of my dreams. It's finally time for all of us to be seen and heard.

EVERY DAY I CHOOSE
TO SURRENDER
ANY CONDITIONING
THAT MIGHT STIFLE
MY WILD. I WORK
TO DETOX MY
DOMESTICATION ONE
LAYER AT A TIME,
AND AS I PEEL AWAY
THE ONION, I FIND
MORE AND MORE OF
MYSELF THAT I'VE
HIDDEN AWAY.

LEA PICKARD

LEA PICKARD

Lea Pickard is a mama, avocado lover, and nontoxic living expert. She helps women create healthier, more sustainable, more natural lives so that their families can thrive and feel wildly free—body, mind, and soul.

Website: https://www.leapickard.com/

FB/IG: https://www.instagram.com/lea.rewild/

To my partner in adventure, Doug: you are the heartbeat of our home and the solid rock to my flowing river. To my lizard-loving jungle boy, Jack: I'm so grateful you remind me daily to stay wild. Thank you both for always supporting my dreams.

CHAPTER 10

REMEMBER YOUR WILD

But darling, you were always wilder than the wind,
you are made of woman.

-Unknown

My bathing suit is only halfway up my torso, the ruffle on the sleeve grazing my belly button. My father, looking like a tanned, Sicilian Adonis, is trying to wrangle the sleeve up my arm. But the waves on Waikiki Beach tempt me.

I'm three years old and we're living in Hawaii, where I've spent all my life up to this point. The sand of the Hawaiian beaches is my playground, and no bathing suit can tame my wild. I manage to escape my dad's wrangling and run, as only a toddler can do, straight toward the water.

My mom, who's been documenting this on camera, laughs loudly. I grab sand by the fistful, splash my feet in the water, and manage to take off my bathing suit before my dad finally catches up to me.

Fast-forward two years. My father, who's in the United States Air Force, is now stationed in the Philippines. It's only 8:30 in the morning, and I'm already wearing black embroidered cowboy boots and a white tutu. I'm bound and determined to create my very own concert in my backyard. The sugarcane field behind the house is my backdrop, and my nipa hut—a small playhouse made in traditional Filipino construction—my stage.

I drag the microphone with the long cord through the screened-in patio. My mother has had a mural of a lush jungle scene inspired by Henri Rousseau's surrealist painting *The Dream* painted on one wall, and I notice the tiger's eyes peeking out at me. Finally, I make my way into the sunshine and look up at the clouds moving through the sky. With soft grass under my feet, I begin to belt out a popular song I'd made my own: "I'm a Rhinestone Cowgirl." My dad strums the Glen Campbell chords on his Hummingbird guitar. I start spinning, the tulle of the tutu bouncing in rhythm to my movement. Arms outstretched, I spin so fast that I'm out of control, lose my balance and collapse on the ground in giggles.

When I'm seven, we move to a house in the woods on the Mississippi Gulf Coast. I make my way into my own personal jungle . . . eerily similar to the mural on our wall in the Philippines. Only this time, I'm the one peeking out from the forest, jumping over streams, befriending tadpoles, and spending hours inspecting magnolia leaves. My grandfather, an extraordinary hobby carpenter, builds me a swing that launches over the stream. I pump my legs to go higher and higher, feeling the breeze in my long sandy-blonde hair.

Every one of these moments felt so *natural*. I'd like to say I felt free, but it's only in hindsight I can say how free I truly was. At the time, I was like a fish in water. I didn't actually notice that freedom was the air I breathed. Can you remember what it feels like to be free? Freedom— what an irony to value this concept so deeply and yet to actually feel it so infrequently. These are some of my first memories, memories of a soul so wild it seemed she could never be tamed. Memories of being wild, happy, and free.

LIFE, DOMESTICATED

As I grew, these moments of freedom became so much more fleeting. My childhood freedom was now being interrupted by moments of *domestication*. And most of us remember those moments of being domesticated just as clearly as the fleeting moments of feeling most free. The times when we were told that we were "not enough" or were "too much." The times when we were metaphorically asked to lock away a piece of our wild, to hide a piece of ourselves and become something that we're not.

An offhanded comment from a caretaker. The teasing from a class-mate. A report card from a teacher that said you talked too much. And perhaps even more heart-wrenching, the moments that *we began to believe* others' stories, expectations, and judgments of ourselves. When we became the ones taming our own spirit.

I'm twelve, and I'm standing in my kitchen in Mississippi. The entire wall facing the back of the house is glass. I'm looking at the woods from inside, because somewhere around this time, I had actually stopped spending time *in* nature. I see a mama cardinal, mostly brown with a spray of red burgundy across her face. A raccoon climbs down a tree that touches the back deck, followed by three little bandit-eyed babies. I imagine the toads, tadpoles, snakes, and other wildlife in their wooded ecosystem.

I look down to the white laminated countertop to see what's sitting next to me: a meal replacement shake. (The ads for this brand were everywhere in the '80s, promising to help us shed weight.) As I stand in the kitchen with the shake in my hand, for a fleeting moment the stark contrast between these two things becomes very obvious. Could this really be how we're meant to live? Shrinking ourselves, paying someone else for a meal in a can, looking out at nature from inside four walls? But it's just that—fleeting. I pop the top and lift the can.

When did the unspoken rules become so familiar to me that I began to mistake them as truth?

Get smaller. Take up less space. Shrink your thoughts and your body to make others more comfortable. This is domestication, and it happened so slowly that I didn't even notice it. Somewhere, I actually relinquished my wild and started following these "rules." And these unspoken rules telling us to get smaller require an ecosystem to flourish, and that ecosystem is also small and limiting. While nature is spacious, expansive, uncontrollable, and free, the ecosystem inside requires contraction. Inside, there's only so much space to take up or control, and yet there are so many things to do. Wild means *being*, domesticated means *doing*.

Once I visited the Outer Banks of North Carolina where feral horses run free. When you look across the water, you'll see them running at top speed, wild, with their manes flying behind them. It's hard to imagine them anywhere but right where they are. In one poignant way, we are just like these horses: their bodies evolved for this freedom. Their bodies evolved to take up space, for wild movement. So, it's no wonder that horses, when tamed, often have physical and mental consequences similar to other domesticated animals: strange and unnatural behaviors like repetitive motions or gnawing, change in hormone levels and neurotransmitters, and even evidence of changing genetic expression that make animals that have been domesticated more prone to disease. Scientists call these phenomena among domesticated animals Domestication syndrome.

Wild animals, when domesticated, get sicker. How appropriate is it then that "broken" is the term used to describe taming a wild animal? And indeed, my own body had felt broken. Around the same age that I began that first diet, my body began to express a host of physical symptoms that carried on into adulthood. Along with body dysmorphia and disordered eating, there were ear infections, sinusitis, appendicitis, allergies, chronic back pain, thyroid problems, hormone imbalance, urinary tract infections, and infertility.

It's an unfortunate laundry list that's all too common among women, along with anxiety, depression, overwhelm, and exhaustion. And yet, we've come to believe *common* means *normal*. But neither disease or dis-ease is any more normal for us than it would be for a wild horse that's been broken into domestication.

But what if we're not broken at all? What if, instead, we're simply experiencing the dis-ease of wild beings who've been domesticated? Who've been ripped from nature? What if, like a wild horse that has been broken, we're simply living out of alignment with how we've been designed? What if the pattern of ill health that we experience starting in childhood is our very own version of Domestication syndrome?

If this is true, why don't we notice it? One possible answer is that it happens so slowly that we don't even notice our deficit of wild anymore. Slowly, we chip away at our wild until we come to believe nature is completely separate from us, so much so that we've literally written ourselves out of nature, nature meaning the collective physical world of plants and animals and other features/products of the earth, as opposed to humans, according to one dictionary.

As opposed to humans?

As long as we live in opposition to nature, we will always be at war with ourselves. Sure, our cultural stories and experiences give us powerful guidelines by which we can function, but they can also be so powerful as to blind us to what is true: we, too, are wildlife. We, too, are animals, evolved over millennia in natural habitats with physiology meant for us to thrive in nature. And just like other wild animals, to be tamed requires breaking down our true nature.

SPINNING

It's April 18: a Wednesday, three days after my forty-fourth birthday. I blink my eyes open to see the four posts of the bed. It's a day like any other day. I'm a college professor, my dad's dream for me. Like other Wednesdays before, I'll drive to the liberal arts college where I teach, hold office hours, and grab my purple pen to grade papers on medical anthropology. I roll over and swing my legs over the edge of the mattress. The bed is high, and my legs are short, so I slide down to the ground, planting my feet on the floor.

Suddenly I'm on a roller coaster. I feel as if my body is spinning violently out of control: the blue of the ceiling, the room around me, and the bed are all swirling together into one. I collapse to the floor. I try to stand but am greeted with *even more* vertigo. I crawl across the beige carpet to the door and call loudly for my husband who, along with my five-year-old son, Jack, come running.

You know those pivotal days in your life? The "first day of the rest of your life" moments? This day was one of those days. Though I didn't know it yet, this was the first day of a new path in my life. A seismic shift in *who* I would become, *what* I would do, and *how* I would live.

A few weeks after this day, having been to an ENT, audiologist, endocrinologist, neurologist, and internist, nothing had changed. I'd peed in cups, given blood, done inner ear manipulation, had hearing and vision tests, and even underwent an MRI to check whether I had a brain tumor. But still no answers. I was officially a woman with a mystery illness.

My vertigo made most things in life difficult, as I couldn't walk, drive, or work. I couldn't eat because I was so nauseated. I couldn't look at a computer, get myself to campus, or teach classes. A college professor whose lectures end with her lying on the ground? Probably not the best idea. I was forced to take the rest of the semester off. So, what happened next felt like it was adding insult to injury.

I'm outside on our porch on a sunny day for the first time in days, watching Jack play at his water table, light filtering through the leaves of the tall oak behind him. My husband is home from his nine-to-five during lunch to check on me. Mothering on most days now that I'm home full time with vertigo feels nearly impossible. I look up at him, standing next to me, and I notice how long his hair has gotten. I let the warmth of the sunshine envelop me and close my eyes. Suddenly a thought invaded my mind: *a tornado is about to destroy our house and kill my son.*

I open my eyes, and it's still sunny. There is literally not a cloud in the sky. And yet the thought remains, beginning to get bigger and bigger and now playing on repeat until there is no room for anything else. Eventually, it gets so big that it erupts out. I shout, "Something terrible is going to happen!" The thought completely consumes me until I'm totally lost within my first ever panic attack.

Wasn't it enough that the mystery illness had taken my body, my ability to move, and my livelihood? That it felt like my body had betrayed me? Now it had hijacked my mind too—the thing perhaps most valued by an academic? The moment began a descent into more and more symptoms and months and months of doctor visits that yielded no answers. A descent that became so dark and painful that I no longer wished to live in my body. At my worst, I looked at my husband and said with tears welling in my eyes that I no longer wanted to be alive. I had no idea what to do and couldn't imagine going on.

BROUGHT TO MY KNEES

And then a sacred moment came my way. I'm sitting in the garage, hands full of yellow, green and blue Legos. Jack shuffles around little Lego vehicles on his train table. I'm watching him intently, enjoying the magic of simply being in this moment. Suddenly I feel everything become heavier and foggier, as if I couldn't lift a limb even if you'd pay me a million dollars. I'd been learning over my months of mystery illness that this meant that I'm just about to go spinning into vertigo.

I do my best to mumble something to Jack. "Mommy will be back." I begin to crawl through the house, across the light oak hardwood floors of the living room, and into the beige-carpeted bedroom, the same one where the vertigo all started months before. All the windows are closed. As I reach the base of the bed, I collapse, start spinning, and begin to sob. I hear Jack in the living room crying and asking, "What's wrong with Mommy?" And where am I when my baby boy needs me to answer this question? I've crawled away from him to lie on the floor in a dark room, alone, weeping. More tears come.

Out of the corner of my eye, I see a flash across my phone. A notification from iPhone's podcast app of the week's new podcasts. And for some reason, even though I'm lying in a puddle, I feel compelled to listen to one called *The Good Life Project*. When I open it and begin listening, I hear words from Sri Mati that will change my life.

"If you're really blessed, you'll be given a sacred moment at least one time in your life . . . when you are on your knees. When everything you thought you were falls away and you are only left with what really matters."

"Wait," I said to myself, "did she say on your knees?" Because I was on my knees, literally, right then. And like a light bulb had turned on, a camera flashed, or a lightning bolt lit up a night sky, I could suddenly see. A flood of knowing filled my body.

In that moment, with piercing clarity, I knew that my vertigo, my mystery illness, my dis-ease, was a gift. That this actually *was* my moment on my knees. It was my glorious opportunity to strip away everything that *was not me.*

And in the truth of what remained, I could see little me, that girl who frolicked on the beach, sang at the top of her lungs, and adventured in the woods in her backyard. I remembered what it was like to feel wild and free. And I knew I wasn't broken.

It was in that sacred moment that I decided I must become my own healer. To trust what I knew. I knew that there was something inside me that didn't belong. Something that was blocking my true nature and my body's innate ability to heal. After doctor after doctor misdiagnosing me or telling me there was nothing wrong with me, I would eventually discover that my body was full of black mold, heavy metals, and toxic chemicals. I was being poisoned, which had led to disease of the mitochondria inside my cells that are supposed to power every system inside my body . . . but weren't. My body was toxic.

I hadn't listened when my body whispered repeatedly for years and years, and now my body was, rightly, screaming for help. My body wasn't actually broken at all; my body was warning me that *I had been broken.*

I knew that domestication had made me sick. If my illness had been caused by a deficit of nature, my healing would happen by returning to the wild . . . at least as much as one could do when one lives in the suburbs in Mississippi. I played outside for hours a day, bathed in sunlight, took long walks on meandering paths in nature, foraged for local flora, grew my own herb garden, planted my feet firmly on the earth, and watched as many fiery, golden sunsets as possible. My life became my medicine.

REMEMBERING WILD

I call my healing process *rewilding.* In ecology, rewilding describes the restoration of an ecosystem to its natural form so that native flora and fauna can once again thrive. Rewilding projects have recreated ecosystems and allowed reintroduction of animals driven from their once natural habitat, like the gray wolf in Yellowstone National Park or the wild Konik horses on the plains of Croatia. The goal of rewilding as described by the conservationist who coined the term? *Restore wildness to nature.*

And slowly, just like the rewilding projects to reintroduce animals into their natural habitats, wildness began to take root in my body again, and I healed. For more than a year I felt like my life had been in a vice grip, twisting and ripping my body and mind into a million pieces. Yet over the course of just a few months of rewilding, every symptom I had been dealing with because of toxicity and mitochondrial damage disappeared. And for the first time since my first diet, I fell back in love with my body. And I truly, deeply remembered what freedom felt like.

Remembering how to be wild again was my homecoming. I felt better than I ever had in my entire life. And it's no wonder why. It's certainly no coincidence that the root of "heal" comes from the Old English *haelen*, meaning "to make whole."

I'd reunited with the wild parts of myself that I'd hidden away. I'd remembered what already lived within me.

I was whole.

But let's be clear: I didn't actually *choose* to rewild. The wild already lived within me, and when I was left on my knees and everything else was stripped away, I could simply see it again. I didn't *choose* to go out into nature. I *am* nature. Rewilding simply helped me rediscover that nature lives within me.

But I did make intentional choices. When I sat with my father as he took his last breath right after I'd begun to heal, I chose to stay wild. I chose to never again lock pieces of myself away or to live my life meeting domestication's standard. I chose to continue the rewilding that changed my life and brought me back to myself. So, I sold my house in Mississippi, and my family moved to the beach where we could be barefoot with our feet in the sand and move our bodies in the sunshine. Because sometimes rewilding means being willing to leave behind a place you have known, maybe even a place you have become very comfortable, for a place that is *truer to your nature*.

Rewilding also means trusting the hunger that lives within. Our hearts are not meant to lock away our dreams and desires, they are meant to crack wide open to light and possibility. So, I ended my career as an academic and started a business that I love. A business birthed as I spoon-fed my father his final meal in his earthly body: chocolate coconut ice cream. A business to help others remember that the wild that saved my life also lives within them.

Every day I choose to surrender any conditioning that might stifle my wild. I work to detox my domestication one layer at a time, and as I peel away the onion, I find more and more of myself that I've hidden away. I make my life my medicine. I resigned from academia—someone else's dream—to live my own. My illness helped me see just how many women were also struggling with symptoms they couldn't explain, lack of energy or motivation, and *dis-ease*. So now I support other women in living a nontoxic, more natural lifestyle by helping them remove toxins from their bodies and their homes. Together, we work to create safer, more sacred spaces where their wild can thrive. My business is changing lives, and I feel so aligned now that I am living my purpose.

I walk with my family on the white sand beach at sunset every night. One evening, with blue-green sea-glass waves lapping at our feet, I looked out at the sky and saw a storm rolling in. There was a time when I hid from storms. But on this hot and steamy night, I watched the layers of gray clouds marbling the sky with thunder clouds get closer and closer. Raindrops began to bead on our skin and roll off into the ocean water. There is a past version of me that wanted to run from this rain. But present me knows a wild truth. Every night the sun will set, and the night will descend. And every morning the sun will rise again. Out of the darkness, the light is born. Nature makes no mistakes. Even the biggest storms bring a glorious gift: rebirth. Present me asks, "Who will I be on the other side?"

Note: While disease usually refers to an illness of the body accompanied by physical symptoms, dis-ease occurs when the body is in a state of disharmony, or *not at ease*. Based on mind-body principles from cultures around the globe, we know the two are often deeply intertwined.

YOU KNOW, THE LOTUS FLOWER, IT GROWS IN MUDDY AND DIRTY SWAMP WATERS. YET IT RISES AND EMERGES THROUGH THE MURKY WATER AND BLOOMS ABOVE IT, PURE AND WHITE, UNTOUCHED BY THE UGLINESS THAT IT GREW OUT OF.

LUSIANA LUKMAN

LUSIANA LUKMAN

As a third-generation teacher, Lusiana Lukman has been teaching piano in Canada since 1991. Her mastery and love for teaching inspired her to start the Classical Music Conservatory (CMC) in Toronto in 1997. CMC is dedicated to helping students with their long-term music goals through their high-quality instruction and nurturing team. Lusiana holds ARCTs with honors in Piano Performance and Pedagogy, a Bachelor of Music, and a Master of Music in Composition. Lusiana lives in Toronto with her spouse and business partner, Wanda, where they've raised their three children together.

Website: www.cmccanada.com

FB/IG: @cmccanada97 @birucalamari

Dedicated to those who have been touched and left in the dark in silence. Know that nothing you did or did not do was the cause of what happened to you. Get help, talk to someone, heal and be whole. You are worth it.

CHAPTER 11

THE LOTUS FLOWER

"So, you want to change piano teachers?" That was all the response I got from the person I had just nervously confided in at the conservatory I was attending that the piano teacher who had taught me for more than two years had repeatedly violated me during my lessons with him.

I was fifteen years old the very first time that piano teacher touched my breasts from behind. I was shocked and frozen to the core. I truly did not know why it was happening. He was so old and frail looking. *Is he losing his mind?* I asked myself. Then, he just moved on like nothing had happened, talking about the piano piece I had just played for him, and my "regular" piano lesson continued.

I didn't say anything to anyone after that first time. I barely spoke English, having grown up in Jakarta, Indonesia. I had come to Canada on my own only months earlier as a new immigrant. I couldn't verbalize what had happened. I was shocked. Then it happened again, weeks later, and again I was stunned and embarrassed. I pushed his hand aside with my elbow and shrugged him off, not being sure what else to do or say. Again, he just kept on with the lesson, saying, "You know, you just really have to practice more; you'd go very far with your talent." In my mind, my thoughts were mushy; nothing was making any sense. Everything was becoming an anxiety-inducing trigger.

I started having nightmares. I felt like I was being choked in my sleep. I didn't associate the nightmares at that time with the sexual abuse that was happening to me. I blamed myself, thinking I must be doing something wrong. I had just started developing a relationship with a girl, and my having grown up in a fundamentalist Christian household back in Indonesia, I related my nightmares to being punished for that. *Of course, I'm getting nightmares*, I thought to myself. *I'm a terrible Chinese daughter and a sinful Christian. God is punishing me for being gay.*

The abuse went on for a few years, and I somehow managed to put up with it. The teacher would open his metal cabinet door in his studio just wide enough to block the view from the small glass window at the door so no one could see what was happening inside. Every time he did that, my heart would sink, as I knew what it meant.

One day, near the end of my piano lesson, the teacher asked me to look at something near his desk. This was different. I stood up from the piano and walked over, not thinking I had to defend myself. He stared at me, smiled, and said, "I have something for you in my pocket."

I replied, "What is it?"

"It's something you'd like," he said.

"No, it's okay," I said.

I suddenly realized that this was a dangerous situation and started to back away, but it was too late. He grabbed both of my hands firmly, swiftly pulled me toward him and lowered my hands into his pants pockets. I had never realized how strong he was, and I tried to pull back, but I could not. I then realized he was making me stroke his already hard penis. I felt sick to my stomach. My head was spinning, and I am not sure if I said anything, but I do remember trying to pull my hands away but being unable to.

"This is what you should do to your boyfriend," he said.

I don't think I was able to say anything, but I did manage to free my hands, somehow.

"Look, here are some rare stamps I have for you." He pulled his hands out of his pants, then waved some stamps around. I had made the mistake some point earlier in the year of telling him I collected rare stamps.

"It's okay, I don't really have time to collect stamps anymore," I said.

"Take them, I saved them, especially for you, you know."

I managed to get free somehow. I grabbed my books, took the stamps, stupidly, and said, "See you next week, thank you."

Why was I so weak and meek? Who was that person? That is not who I am. I knew it was wrong. Everything about it was wrong. That was my last lesson with him. I was so ashamed that I was not able to say things to him at that time or kick him or do anything else that would have been genuinely better than the soft-spoken response I made to a horrible situation. No one at any music lesson, or at any time or anywhere for that matter, should have had to go through that.

That evening, I told my then-girlfriend all the things that had happened. "You have to tell someone, you have to report him, you have to do something about this," she told me.

"What if he has a heart attack and dies if I tell on him?" I asked. He was over eighty years old at that point in time. Why was I, as a victim, trying to protect this person who had molested me at my piano lessons for years? I was so mad at myself about this for a long time. I felt victimized and robbed.

When I finally got the courage to meet with the person in charge and report my teacher, I thought that if anyone would be able to do something about the abuse, surely this person would do the right thing and ensure this man was stopped. Surely they would make sure this would never happen to anyone else.

I was *wrong*. It was a very difficult meeting. I sat there feeling sick to my stomach in having to talk about the abuse. I felt weak, scared, and alone, and I needed this leader to affirm I was doing the right thing by telling him about it and that something would be done about this teacher. Instead, I was barely acknowledged.

"So, you want to change piano teachers?" was the only response I got, and the meeting ended quietly and quickly. He did not ask any questions about what happened, how long it was happening, or if I needed help to deal with this trauma. There was no paperwork filed to report any of the incidents, only a form to change piano teachers. I went home feeling defeated, unseen, unheard, and unvalued. I later found out that my teacher had been abusing students for fifty years prior to abusing me. I also found out there were other teachers who had been known to have sexually abused their students without any repercussions at all at this school.

GETTING HELP

After a couple of years of trying to move on, going to therapy, and continuing my studies with another piano teacher, I had a run-in with my abuser. I happened to be on the elevator of the music school, and just as the doors were closing, he slipped in. The two of us were alone, and my heart was pounding. He looked straight at me and ominously said, "You know, the things I did, they were for your own good, right? So you can feel things because I cared for you." I said nothing and left the elevator as soon as the doors opened.

I was shaken by that incident and continued to feel disturbed and disillusioned by the situation. I had to keep picking up the pieces so I could move on. I sought help from friends, therapists, and the pastor of my then-church. I have been seeing a therapist since I was eight years old, and I am so grateful that I have. I think everyone should have a therapist in the same way that everyone has a dentist and an eye doctor. After all, our mind is the most important part of our being. We see the dental hygienist at least twice a year, so why aren't we having mental health checkups regularly?

I started to dream that if I had the means later on, I would build a music school that would do better. In fact, I wanted to have a school that would do its best for the students, to guide them in earnest to achieve their individual musical goals in a safe and nurturing environment.

As a visa student, I had to continue my studies in order to stay in Canada. I knew I did not want to go back to Indonesia, as being gay was still illegal there. The moment I landed in Toronto, I felt that I belonged here, that this was where I was meant to be. So, I stayed. I finished my ARCT (a diploma equivalent at the college level) in both piano performance and pedagogical studies in the same year, then applied for my residency in Canada as soon as I could.

Basically, I just had to keep going. The process of healing is never an easy or a quick one. It was hard enough being a teenager living away from my parents, but I also had the burden of explaining why I had to succeed added to that. My mind was always trying to consolidate the knowledge of who I was with the obligation of what I was told I had to be. It was a battle between what I was taught in my upbringing and being aware of who I was ever since I was very young.

TEACHING PIANO

I started teaching private piano lessons when I was seventeen. Since I was studying piano pedagogy, I was allowed to teach as part of my studies. I love teaching. I am a third-generation teacher. My grandmother was a math and music teacher, my mother was a piano teacher, and my uncle was a violin teacher. I started to see how a good teacher can make a positive impact on the lives of students.

Things didn't just come to fruition for me right away. I was still young, in my twenties. I was in a very rocky relationship at that time, and my mind was not clear. Life was complicated. I continued to feel very conflicted about being gay, being a Christian, being Chinese, being a foreigner, and wanting to do all the right things in all areas of my life. I was in love with someone who did not want to be open about our relationship. I was unsure about many things, but what I was sure of was that I wanted to be successful, to not have a nine-to-five job, and to not have a boss. I was also sure I had to do things for myself, as I couldn't rely on others to make things happen for me.

I had done one thing right: I had started saving and investing my money when I was eighteen. I had also read many books about investing and business. When I was growing up in Indonesia, my mom was a musician and an emotional person, and my dad was a businessman who was good with money. He had looked down on my mother for her lack of financial know-how, and it was painful to see that in my childhood and early teen years. I promised myself at that time that I would be good with money. I did not want to be like my mother who worked seven days a week but always struggled financially. My parents were never married, so my dad did not live with us. He had his own family. I was told that our situation was different, that my mother was the "other" woman. Thus, we couldn't rely on my dad financially. It was just the way it was.

After teaching piano lessons for a few more years, I felt there was a lot more I could learn about music. I realized performing was not my path, but I could improve myself further as a teacher if I went back to school. I have always loved the theory of music, but I'm not a theorist. As I started taking advanced harmony lessons again, my harmony teacher encouraged me to start composing. After a year of that, he told me he was going to retire. So, I decided to do a music composition degree at the University of Toronto. It was very different and exciting. I loved the process of composing. It taught me a lot more about music and opened my eyes to music like never before. It was very satisfying.

Emotionally, I felt like this was the beginning of my personal growth to becoming whole and clear. I'd always known who I was and what I wanted, but I had to come to terms with how I was able to authentically be myself with my parents' cultural and religious expectations having been drilled into me since birth. I continued to seek the truth for what it is: that God is loving and not small-minded.

This was around the time when I got to my third year, a time when university students start thinking about what to do next after they get their degree. I was teaching about forty students and really enjoyed my composition studies. I had a full life, but I also realized I needed to grow more. I started thinking about starting a music school again.

OPENING THE SCHOOL

As luck would have it, two of my colleagues from the faculty of music started talking about possibly joining me in making this music school a reality. I knew nothing about how to start and build a business in

Canada, and Google did not exist yet. Everything we did was from scratch. It took us from January to August of 1997 to solidify everything from start to finish. At the same time, we were continuing with our university course load, and I was still teaching from my home six days a week, ensuring my income and cash flow continued.

I was in a suburb of Toronto at that time, and most of the friends I wanted to hire were living in Toronto, so we searched and found a great location near the city. I liked the vibe of the place and the fact that it didn't need a lot of renovations. When we were ready to sign the lease, one of my business partners looked at it and said to me, "Um, the lease is for five years! I don't know what I'll be doing in a year!" The other partner agreed with him right away.

"I do!" I said. "This business! If you don't think you are going to still be doing this in a few years, then I don't think you should be in this business."

All of a sudden, my two partners wanted out, and I had to buy them out to proceed. I came up with three times the amount of money to ensure I could open my music school and run it well. I had savings from investing since I was eighteen, but I needed a lot more money than that. Off I went to talk to all the banks I knew in Toronto. Somehow, I was able to get a $30,000 line of credit from a bank, and that was enough money to pay for more than a year's worth of rent if I ended up with no profit from the business. I distinctly remember the phone call I had with the landlord, as he was concerned that now instead of three partners, there was just me signing the five-year lease. "Are you sure you can do this on your own?" he asked me.

I paused for a second, then replied, "Yes, even if we don't have enough students, I have enough money right now to pay the rent for at least a year or so." Somehow, he believed in me, and that was enough for both of us to proceed with the lease.

I started off by moving my students from my home studio to *Classical Music Conservatory* (CMC) for lessons there. I had to do everything on my own for the first five years: getting students, scheduling, calling people, making flyers, advertising, obtaining permits, cleaning, book-keeping—literally everything. I was at the school every hour we were open, and at the same time, I was also finishing my bachelor's degree and then my master's degree. I barely slept, and I had no social life. But this was what I had to do to survive. Looking back, on the one hand, I wish I had known a lot more than I did about starting a business. On the other hand, I feel very lucky I didn't know any better, because if I did, I may not have started my business out of the fear of failure.

COMING FULL CIRCLE

Everyone can do this: you just have to believe in yourself, keep working wisely, get help on things you don't know about, and never give up. Your business needs to be something you're truly passionate about. I love teaching. I love helping students figure things out through music. It's amazing how much about life you can learn through music, as well as how much you can learn the skill of learning through music. It's also very rewarding to be able to see my students weekly for years. Most of our students are with us for more than twelve years, a whole genera-tion really, until they graduate from high school. Many students keep in touch, with some coming back for lessons after university. What's even more beautiful is that some of my students have now brought their own children to CMC for lessons, and that makes me feel so happy. It's profoundly fulfilling.

I also am so blessed that I eventually met the partner I've always wanted in life and business, Wanda. She helped me grow CMC to where it stands today. She brought warmth, beauty, and a homey atmosphere, as well as all the detailed procedures that help everything run smoothly. We complement each other perfectly. We share the vision of caring for students like they are part of our family. We both believe that each student is unique and has their own individualized musical journey. We both want to ensure each student is seen and heard for who they are and that they get the customized guidance that will help them achieve their personal musical goals, whatever they may be.

With Wanda, I also gained three stepchildren who we've raised together at home and at CMC. They have taken multiple instrumental and voice lessons here. Like every family, all three are very different in their musical discipline and approach. Our oldest is now a successful professional musician, touring and making her own music and a great name for herself. Our middle child jams with his friends whenever he can, and our youngest continues to play his cello and the piano whenever he's home from university. I could not have planned our lives together any better. I mean, our kids are even half Asian! They all know and understand my quirks, and I love each of them uniquely.

I remember a special saying that my mom would tell me:

"You know, the lotus flower, it grows in muddy and dirty swamp waters. Yet it rises and emerges through the murky water and blooms above it, pure and white, untouched by the ugliness that it grew out of."

I didn't let my experience of abuse as a young person define me. Instead, I used it to fuel myself to build a great music school that is safe, caring, and gives unparalleled support to our students, parents, and teachers.

Life is full, amazing, and beautiful. I also have come to understand that God is not black and white, that God is the full spectrum of the colors of the rainbow, and that love is love.

I am truly grateful for this great life.

I DON'T HAVE TO DO EVERYTHING ON MY OWN. I'M NOT A BURDEN BECAUSE I ASK FOR HELP. I AM A HUMAN WHO DESERVES SUPPORT, AND I'M STILL AMAZING.

MEAGHAN BEAMES

MEAGHAN BEAMES

Meaghan Beames is a Registered Massage Therapist, a Craniosacral Therapist, and the mother of two young kids, Lincoln and Ruby. She lives in Toronto, Canada, where she runs her two craniosacral businesses and does her very best to try to make the world a better place.

Website: www.mybabycst.com

FB/IG: @mybabycst @beamescst

Thank you to Lianne Kim for opening my eyes to parts of myself I'd never seen before, to my sisters for always having my back, and to my mom for being exactly who I needed her to be in order to be who I am today.

CHAPTER 12

BEING BRAVE IS ASKING FOR HELP

I've always lived in my own little world. Call it naïveté, call it dissociation, call it what you want, but Meaghan Land is a pretty cool place, and I believe that is how I was able to go through life believing I could do anything and that I was amazing, no matter what society might say of me.

My parents separated when I was four years old. I was raised by a beautiful and courageous single mother of three, with me being the youngest. I don't have very many memories from before I was four, and those after are muddled, but I do remember the hot summer drive to the new apartment the day my parents split up. I was in the back seat of a red pickup truck that was borrowed by one of my mom's friends. With my mom sitting next to me, I asked, "Mom, where are we going?"

She replied, "We're moving to a new place and Daddy is going to be living somewhere else." In fact, he was going to live in a dark motel room with an outdoor pool filled with last year's leaves and algae and an AC unit indoors that was so powerful it froze the curtains solid.

I couldn't really comprehend what was happening with my family, as I was so young. I don't remember having any emotion about it. I just took it as fact and went with it. My sisters and I were living with my mom in this apartment, and my dad was living alone in that gross motel room. Cool. Got it. Check.

One of my mom's favorite things to say is: "I hope you don't need therapy because of this." She knew she was doing her best, but she also knew her kids were dealing with a lot of emotions. She put us in a program for kids with divorced parents called "Kids Are People, Too." Best program. I highly recommend it.

Our new apartment was in a government-subsidized building on the other side of town. We had just moved from a four-bedroom home. We used to have a giant backyard with a swing set, a weeping willow tree that would brush the top of my head when I ran under it, and a playroom so packed full of toys you couldn't open the door all the way. Each of us kids had our own room, yet we chose to share one.

I went from living in a quiet neighborhood in the suburbs to living in the inner city. The new place was small. Luckily, sharing a room wasn't an issue for us kids; in fact, it was preferred. We loved each other and never fought. Strange, right? Three sisters who *never ever fought*. Maybe it was because we felt we had to stick together, as our parents were clearly going through hard times before the separation.

Our unit was on the third floor, and there was no elevator. Imagine being a single mom of three small kids and getting them to walk up three flights of stairs every day. My mom would walk ahead and leave the door open for us to finally drag ourselves through when we got to the top. Yeah, that's what I would do too if I were a single mom of three kids under ten.

My sisters and I made friends with the kids in our new building. I remember thinking that these kids seemed a little rough, their clothes weren't as nice as the ones worn by my old friends, and their parents also weren't together, just like mine. Some kids were clearly neglected by their parents.

GROWING UP

It took a year before my mom saved enough money for a down payment on a house. She was so proud, so excited that she was buying a home, but for some reason, she wouldn't tell us where it was! Turns out it was next door to the apartment. The house that was clearly haunted. The house where no kid dared walk on the grass. My mom was proud—we were terrified. It was an old farmhouse, built in 1875, and the wife of the man who built it died in their bedroom. Told ya. *Haunted*.

Moving out of the apartment and into the house next door brought us to a new status level, apparently, even though we were the same three kids and single mother who lived in the apartment next door. I made new friends who had houses down the street. They all had two parents still together, dogs, cats, and hobbies, and they ate dinner as a family.

My next-door neighbor, who became my best friend, had parents that were still married. They had three kids, a dog, and a beaver panel station wagon where you could sit backward in the back seat. They weren't well-to-do, but her grandparents were, and she got *all* the presents at Christmas. Each year, we'd call each other up and talk about what we got. One year, I think we were ten, she got a bass guitar and a speaker. I don't think I ever once saw her play that guitar or turn on that speaker after that Christmas afternoon.

As a kid, I never got the Tickle Me Elmo, the Furby, or the Polly Pockets, but my friends all did. What was also very different was the food. This is where I felt the divide. In grade two, my lunch consisted of a granola bar from my friend. I'm not sure if it was because making lunches was a task that was too much for my stretched-thin mother, or if we just didn't have the food. Either way, I went to school hungry and managed to make it through the school day on about 300 calories. I remember looking at other kids' lunch boxes and thinking, *wow, not only do they have a lunch box, but they have food in it too!* I wished I had those things, but somehow, in my preadolescent mind, I knew my mom was tired, and stressed, and had her own emotional needs that weren't being met. I didn't tell her I needed help with packing lunch. So, I just kept eating the daily granola bars.

I don't for one second blame my mom for anything that was happening in our childhood. She was filled with love, affection, encouragement, and a strong feminist edge, and she gave us everything she could. But sometimes, her resources were low. Resources being time, energy, and emotional support. She did the best she could, and in looking back, I think, *crap, she was a single mom of three girls. That shit is hard.* I couldn't imagine what it would be like to not have a supportive partner. No wonder she would lock herself in her room and tell us she needed her space. We probably drove her nuts! And no wonder we girls felt we needed to take care of ourselves. We didn't want to be a burden on our mom. She had enough going on.

FINDING MY STYLE

Clothes were definitely something that set me apart from the other kids at school. My friends would do fashion shows of the clothes they got from the mall or big stores like The Bay. They'd even talk about how they'd drive down to Toronto because they didn't want to have the same clothes as everyone else. Back-to-school shopping in my house consisted of thrift store shopping and us sifting through giant bags of hand-me-downs, fighting over who was going to get what. We were all pretty much the same size for many years.

Do you remember when store flyers were stuffed into newspapers and dropped off at your door? Yeah, I stuffed those newspapers with flyers from the age of ten to twelve. I got $21 a month and felt like I was rolling in it. I used to look through my favorite stores before painstakingly putting together roughly seventeen flyers, arranging them from biggest to smallest, and stuffing them inside the paper. I can still feel the ink on my hands after handling all that paper. I looked through the flyers with clothes I probably would never have and imagined myself dancing around in them. There was one dress that I just *had* to have. It was one of those stretchy black A-line dresses with white and yellow flowers printed above the waistline. I got the money I had saved for the past two months, went down to BiWay, and I bought myself that dress. I wore that dang dress every day until it ripped, and then I wore it with shorts.

My sisters and I loved vintage shopping before vintage shopping was cool. I used my paper route money to go to our favorite thrift store, where I bought my favorite brown Corduroys, 1970s patterned long lapel button-up, and fifteen soccer shirts . . . I'm not sure who my stylist was back then! Anyway, on picture day, you *know* I wore that shit to school. I strutted my stuff into the lineup to class, and then it happened. The finger pointing, the snickering, the laughing. I wasn't new to being teased for things I wore. So, I held my head high because I was damn proud of my outfit. After all, I was eleven, and I bought it with my own money. But the kids at school thought my clothes were funny. Especially the new girl who had claimed her stake as "most popular girl," only because she had bullied her way there. She stood there, in her brand-new outfit from Sears, with a look of disgust on her face as if my outfit was that offensive. I made the decision at that moment that it didn't matter if the other kids didn't like my clothes, I did, and I would wear what made me feel good. If they didn't want to be my friend because of it, well, they were missing out.

I can still see the look on my face in my school photo. I'm beaming with pride in my button-up shirt with the green-and-blue Monet-style landscape that was printed on repeat throughout, the lapels draped wide over my shoulders.

MAKING IT ON MY OWN

My eldest sister and I were very outgoing, my middle sister, not so much. Penny, the oldest sister, was in a theater group, and I was so envious. I wanted to be up on that stage, dancing, singing, and being the center of attention. My middle sister, Kaity, was happy to be a very active member of the audience; the limelight was not her thing. Penny was in the theater group for a few years before I was old enough to audition for a spot. I planned and rehearsed for my audition and decided I was going to do impersonations. But not just any impersonation. Nooo. None other than the director of the company herself. Why, you ask? Because I have balls of steel? It makes sense now why people were laughing so hard because apparently, I nailed it.

I got in. Yep. They let me in even though I was the youngest person they had ever let into the group, and I had essentially made fun of the director to secure my spot. I'm not sure how my mom paid for my entry fees that year, but the next year, it wasn't the same story. She could only afford to pay the $1,000 a year for one kid, and that was going to be Penny. I was crushed.

I confided in my friend who lived in a country mansion outside of town, her Ford Expedition parked in the driveway, that I would not be joining her the next year because my family didn't have the money. It wasn't uncommon for the kids in the theater company to be from very well-off families, and her house was no exception. I went to some other houses, and none of them had dirt floor basements like I did, or old furnaces that leaked CO_2 and could explode at any moment. They had two-car garages, and pools, and their parents had fancy jobs. My friend's mom, who had essentially taken me in as one of her own, said, "Well, Meaghan, let's get writing." That was my first experience with grant writing.

I wrote a more condensed story in my grant application than what I've shared with you. I poured my heart into this letter, telling them how much I loved to be on stage and that performing for people made me feel good but that my family didn't have the means. I sent off my one-page request for $1,000 to some of the old-timey membership groups like the Shriners Club; the Lions Club; and the Army, Navy, and Air Force Club. It was the Shriners Club that responded with a $1,000 grant for me to get back into the troupe. I was twelve.

The year after that, I paid the fees from the babysitting money I had saved from the year before. I've always been a hustler—willing to take care of what mattered to me. This was around the age when I realized it was up to me to make my own way if there was something I really wanted. It didn't matter that my parents weren't the wealthiest, or that I didn't have a giant house with a bunch of cars. If I wanted something badly enough, I decided that I would find a way to get it. I'm self-sufficient and proud and don't need anyone else to help me.

This was evident when at seventeen, I moved out with my high school sweetheart, started paying rent, and got my first credit card and my first line of credit. I used that to pay for my tuition to hairdressing school. My dad told me a story not too long ago that he didn't even know I had signed myself up for school until one day when I asked him for a ride to my first day of class. He said he was shocked. He had no idea I had plans of going to postsecondary school, but he was proud—proud that

I had made this decision on my own and that I had chosen a trade I felt passionate about.

I was a hairdresser for thirteen years, but I couldn't help but feel like there was more to me, that I needed to help people more profoundly. I decided to go to massage therapy school, and I paid my way through my first two years by working crazy hours as a hairstylist, graduating my last year with only a small percentage of the $15,000 government loan I had started with. I met my partner in massage therapy school. We moved in together and were pregnant six weeks after graduation.

BABIES AND MY CALLING

I love babies. I've always loved babies. At a family gathering, if there was a new baby around, I was holding them, like holding them until their mother asked me to have their baby back. When I had my own baby, it was no different. I trained as a doula, thinking that was the only way I could work with babies. I took this virtual training with my three-month-old nursing at the breast. But the on-call life was not something I wanted. I had a baby that would scream if he couldn't smell my armpit at night. How could I leave him for hours on end?

I learned about craniosacral therapy for babies, and that's when my entire future flashed before my eyes. It was like the dress in the flyer. I loved it, and I had to have it. So, everything I did going forward was toward taking craniosacral therapy training in a different country. Yes. That's right. I was in Toronto, Canada, and the training was in Portland, Oregon. It was thousands of miles away.

Then I got pregnant. Again. And my dream of taking the course faded, as saving for a new addition to the family became the priority. But it didn't last long. I could feel that pull toward my calling, and I couldn't deny it. I signed up for the class while I was six months pregnant, knowing I would be taking my three-month-old baby with me. I prayed to have a baby that didn't scream all the time.

Additionally, I asked my mom to come with me to Portland to help. That took a lot of effort for me to do. I thought for sure I was going to do it on my own, but I stepped out of my comfort zone instead.

When I came back home, my friend and new business partner at the time started running our business. I felt I couldn't do it on my own because who was I? I wasn't a business owner. I wasn't savvy enough to run a business of this caliber by myself. For the first two years, the effort and priorities in the business were very one-sided, and I was on the side with the higher priorities in the business. I did all the things: creating the website, making connections within the community, and taking as many clients as possible, but I couldn't have the hard conversation with my business partner about how I was feeling. I couldn't ask for help. Remember my theme? I can do it all. It's okay, I got this. I won't be a burden. I don't need help.

TRANSITIONS

I worked myself into a depression. I wasn't sleeping at night, I wasn't treating my family well, I was taking my anger out on my kids, and I just wasn't happy with the way things were going with the business. Then the pandemic happened, and our business was forced to close temporarily, the business partnership dissolved, and I had a miscarriage. Talk about hitting rock bottom. I had to make a decision: it was either me or my business, and we couldn't both survive the way we were going. So, I made the decision to reevaluate my role and chose to ask for help. I realized I was worthy of having someone else do the work—I don't have to do everything for this business to stay afloat. I thought I needed another revenue-generating employee, but what I really needed was for someone to take over the admin work. So, over the summer I made it my mission to hire an admin assistant, and for two years now I have never not had someone working for me.

Hiring isn't easy. I have found it very difficult. There is always this little voice in me that says, "But if you hire someone, and they stay with you long enough, they'll learn the real you, and then they'll quit." This is something I am working on with my therapist. I know that it is my inner child voice I've kept to myself. It's closed me off from allowing others in, and I'm not allowing myself to be vulnerable and accept help. Or even ask for it.

I know this is the voice of the little girl who felt it was up to her to make her way; it was up to her to not need anyone to do things for her, to defend herself, or to fight for what she wanted.

I continue to fight for what I want, but I do it with help. I show gratitude to my employees, and I show them all the sides of me. I'm still apologizing for the sides I don't like, as if that will help them to stay. I'm doing the work now to know that no matter what side I show to people, I am always worthy of help, and that if someone chooses to leave the business, it isn't about me. They have their own lives, their own problems, their own things they are dealing with daily. I am always grateful for whoever comes in and out of my business, because they all teach me something.

I'm so incredibly proud of myself and my transformation. Not only have I built two businesses that are designed to better the lives of families who are struggling with their babies, but I've learned about who I am. I've bettered my own life by working through childhood traumas, parenting my inner child, and creating a mindset of "I've got this because I have the support behind me to do it!"

I don't have to do everything on my own. I'm not a burden because I ask for help. I am a human who deserves support, and I'm *still* amazing.

Owning a business is more than just growing an entity or building a brand. It is about doing the inner work, and it is about parenting your inner child and growing emotionally.

I HAD HEARD PEOPLE SAY THAT SUCCESS WASN'T LINEAR, BUT I HAD NO IDEA.

SAMANTHA VLASCEANU

SAMANTHA VLASCEANU

Samantha Vlasceanu, The TikTok Coach, is on a mission to convince businesses and brands that TikTok is not just for our teenagers (and no dancing is required)! Samantha works with marketing agencies, coaches, lawyers, corporate brands—you name it! She ensures all her clients are using the app with intention as a sales funnel in finding their target audience, and she teaches them the strategies of converting their followers into ACTUAL paying clients.

Website: www.thetiktokcoach.ca

FB/IG: @TheTikTokCoach

To Ethan, Harper, and Mihai. For always catching me when I fall.

CHAPTER 13

FAIL NOW TO SUCCEED TOMORROW

I had heard people say that success wasn't linear, but I had no idea. The "plan" has changed, dipped, twisted, turned around, and flipped upside down so many times that it's completely unrecognizable. Each turn has had its share of hurt, failure, shame, and more. But each turn got me to where I am today. I thought it would be simple for me because I had a plan: I would go to Ivey Business School and climb the corporate ladder. And so, according to said plan, I was accepted to Richard Ivey School of Business in London, Ontario, one of the most prestigious business schools in Canada.

Have you ever gone somewhere, walked in the door, then realized everyone was dressed more formally than you? That's what Ivey felt like to me. I was with A-type personalities whose parents owned major brands or were CEOs of big-time retailers. Who was I to be in the same room as these people who had been raised by people making serious moves in the business world? Of course, they were at Business School. They probably had stock exchange bedtime stories and business in their blood. I felt completely out of place. I didn't speak the same language of investment banking and business. It felt like I was at the same party, but only because someone made a mistake with the guest list. I lacked real connections—people who simply got me.

It was lonely and hard, but it was "the dream." When I didn't feel like I belonged, I pushed it aside. When I didn't feel like I was "getting it" or "smart," I just kept grinding. Because while it didn't feel right, it was the *plan*. I was going to graduate from Business School and climb the corporate ladder, no matter the cost.

After graduation, that feeling only grew. I went for interview after interview, only to not be chosen for the job. It seemed like the business world was confirming what I knew to be true—that I didn't belong. I felt like I was failing, but I eventually landed in management consulting as an analyst.

I did that job for ten years, and I did well at it. If I questioned whether it was the right career for me, my family quickly shut down that talk. I had a well-paying job with good benefits. What else did I want? They were right to an extent—I did have a job many others wanted. But I wasn't happy. I wasn't fulfilled. This didn't feel like success. It didn't feel right.

I watched my friends climbing the corporate ladder, becoming directors and VPs, and starting businesses. They were moving forward; I was standing still. Not only did it not feel right, but the "dream" plan was not going the way I thought it would. I was quickly falling behind my peer group in a field that didn't even excite me. I wasn't moving forward, but there didn't seem to be any way to move faster. It also didn't seem like there was any other path to take. I felt stuck, disillusioned, and disheartened. Was this it for me? To stay in a job that I felt lukewarm about and just flounder in middle management?

My dissatisfaction grew, and I could feel depression sinking its claws into me. I felt like everyone else was riding this wave, but I had missed it. It felt more like I missed the whole ocean! The culture I grew up in did not talk about mental health. While my family loves me unquestionably, they were ill-equipped to help me during this time. My husband tried to comfort me, pointing out that being a mom was its own accomplishment. My friends were too busy living their own versions of success. On top of having all these emotions, I had nowhere to turn for support.

Even though I had not "failed" (I still had a job, after all), I felt like a failure. Thankfully, it was all about to change because I was going to start a business. I had been traveling with my children and wanted to combine that with my business acumen. It was the move I was convinced would be a game changer—Traveling Munchkin.

TRAVELING MUNCHKIN

In my mind, it was a genius idea: an Airbnb model for baby gear. In my mind, it was going to go Canada-wide and then global. I had a blind spot the size of a traveling munchkin, but no one was going to convince me that this wasn't the best idea anyone had ever had. I was so adamant that this was it.

My in-laws tried to convince me that it wouldn't work out. My father-in-law even broke down the math for me: for every $100 order, I would only make a $20 commission. I would have to sell 1,000 orders to make $20,000 per year. They tried to reason with me: what about insurance? Liability? Is the time you're spending away from your kids worth it?

And my parents? They didn't even recognize it as a business. To them, it was a hobby, albeit a weird one. My incredibly supportive husband felt like it wasn't a long-term career, but he was happy that I was happy. However, to him, it was a passion project.

No one saw it but me. But I worked hard, strived at it, dedicated every spare waking moment to it, and it was picking up. It was a grind, but there was movement. In early 2020, I consistently got a couple of orders per day.

COVID-19

In early 2020, it made sense to have a business based on travel. In March 2020, it no longer made sense. COVID-19 brought the entire world screeching to a halt. Travel was locked down. No one knew when (or if) the pandemic would end. So, I put Traveling Munchkin on hold and tried to rally. I thought this would blow over in a month. Two months. Three months.

When it became clear, even to me, that Traveling Munchkin would not be able to operate anytime soon, it was like a dagger to my heart. I was finally doing something that felt interesting, that felt like I was moving, and it was going to be over before it really began. My depression kicked in hard. I felt like everyone was right. No one had ever believed it would succeed, and now they were right.

My parents were right.
My in-laws were right.
My husband was right.

I felt like I had been wrong all along. Wrong to believe that I could be and do more. Again, that lost feeling crept in. Untethered. Unsure what to do next. Stuck between a rock and a hard place. I didn't want to be in my management job, and my escape hatch had just been nailed shut. At the same time, I felt guilty. From the outside looking in, I had it all and I felt guilty that I wasn't more grateful. That I wasn't happy. People were getting sick and dying, and there were way bigger problems out there than my personal satisfaction.

But the fact remained that I was miserable, frustrated, confused, and lonely with all those feelings. At that point, I was so deep into depression that I didn't care about feeling happy. I just wanted to feel okay. That was the low bar I set for myself.

Around that time, in October 2020, I found out I would be laid off from my corporate job. After all the earlier failures, you'd think I would have been knocked down, but I couldn't have been happier! This was the sign I was waiting for—it wasn't bad news. It was an opportunity. I could take a minute and figure out my next steps.

TIKTOK—A TURNING POINT

While dealing with how I felt and the grief surrounding Traveling Munchkin, I found an escape. That escape was TikTok, a short-form video hosting service with downloads in the billions. In life, I couldn't deal. I couldn't handle it. However, on TikTok, I could scroll and be mindlessly entertained. But it wasn't mindless for long. I started to see the value of the platform. Then I began to post some videos to keep Traveling Munchkin afloat (because at that time, I was still in deep denial about the future of that business).

I didn't save my travel business, and that hurt. A lot. But I was gaining traction on TikTok. I was learning about the platform, how its algorithm worked and how to grow a following. I learned how to connect with my audience, which was something I noticed many other businesses ignored. As I grew, businesses began asking me to learn more about marketing their businesses on TikTok.

I enrolled in a group coaching program with Lianne Kim to figure out my next steps. In my mind, I was going to do it all. First, I'd get Traveling Munchkin back (grief is a process—I was still in the denial phase), then I would be an influencer, a consultant, and I would help other businesses with their TikTok marketing.

It became apparent in the first month which idea was going to stick. The more I talked about TikTok, the more I realized businesses needed help. The more I learned about the platform and grew my own presence, the more I saw opportunities for people to build their brands. I was living what I was coaching. I saw what was possible on this platform, and I was helping others see it too. Finally, I felt like I was a success. It finally felt right.

That's not to say it was easy. Telling people that I was trading the corporate ladder for an app known mostly for dancing teenagers? Not easy. Hearing people doubt me, criticize me, and tell me I was wasting my time? Not easy. Having people ask me if it was worth the time I *wasn't* spending with my kids? Not easy and definitely ramped up my mom guilt. But it didn't matter. I was not backing down, and two things were keeping me going. First, I was surrounding myself with other amazing women who got it. They knew why I was working at 2 a.m. on a business that wasn't making big money. They knew why this was so important to me. Why it mattered so much and why I was giving it everything I had.

Second, my gut was telling me that this was right. This was the feeling I had been chasing all along. That feeling unlocked the door to many other things. I could put Traveling Munchkin behind me and appreciate it for what it was: a failed business that taught me so much. The sting of failure didn't hurt quite as much because I could finally see what was ahead. Knowing what was beyond that pain, I could see and be grateful for the lessons I learned. Knowing what that failure was helping me to build instead helped me through my grief so I could accept it and move on.

With Traveling Munchkin, I wasted so much time overthinking colors and fonts. With *The TikTok Coach*, I made decisions faster. I moved faster. My earlier failures showed me that what makes a business successful is not planning, it's *doing*. It's like having kids. The first one you fret over every bump, bruise, cough, and sniffle. The second one . . . not so much.

Without that failure, *Sam the TikTok Coach* would not be here today. Without being forced to pivot, I would still be striving at a business that was never going to work. I now have a business I am proud of and passionate about. I wake up excited every day about what I do and am seeing myself hitting milestones that were once a dream.

SUCCESS / LESSONS LEARNED

My business helps others to realize their dreams. I built a business where my clients pay me for my worth and the value I bring. Not only that, but I also built a support network, business mentors, and people I respect that I had been missing all along.

Finally, I am where I am supposed to be, on the path I am meant to be walking, taking the journey that I have built with my own two hands. When I start talking TikTok and coaching people, I don't just feel okay about it. I feel confident. I am walking in as a different person, not Sam the wife or Sam the mother. I am Sam the TikTok Coach who is about to change your business.

My kids (aged four and six at the time of writing) think I'm the coolest mom in the world! I am the mom who is on TikTok for work! However, I know that won't last forever. Wait a few years until they're old enough to be on the platform too and it's embarrassing for them . . . my cool mom factor will quickly take a nosedive.

To this day, my family still doesn't totally get what I do and why I do it. They don't really see the potential in it, but you know what? That's okay. That confidence that I have—they see that. And that confidence tells me that what matters is that I get it. I see it.

I have also changed my perspective about how my family feels. They love me, and their worry comes from a place of love. They care about me (which I absolutely appreciate), and at the end of the day, they want me to be happy.

When my confidence dips, I think about the results that I have gotten. In fact, one of my corporate clients (a global beauty brand) had to suspend their TikTok marketing because they sold out of their product. My clients have gained millions of followers and have had their businesses explode after working together with me. My clients are achieving results that were once just a dream. And none of this would have ever happened without those first failures. But it's not to say I've gotten all my mishaps out of the way. I still fail, and I know I will continue to experience bumps in the road. One of my first corporate proposals didn't go as planned, in fact.

Does it get me down? A little. I'm still human. But it doesn't get me down for long. Because I know that each failure has a lesson. It will be the story I'll tell in my next chapter—about how I grew even more. If you're experiencing something similar right now, here's what I wish I had known earlier:

1. It's okay not to be okay, even if everyone tells you that you should be.
2. Surround yourself with people who will build you up and not tear you down.
3. Don't see failure as a way to knock you down, see it as a teacher and use it as a place to grow and learn.

Don't give up. Because trust me, one day, it will just feel right. It will feel like success.

PEOPLE TALK ABOUT
DEBT AS CURRENCY,
BUT WHEN YOU BUILD
SOMETHING FROM
NOTHING AND HAVE
THE RIGHT PEOPLE
GIVE A CHAPTER OF
THEIR LIVES TO CARRY
YOUR MISSION AND
YOU CAN NOW NO
LONGER PROVIDE
THAT SUPPORT TO
THEM, THE DEBT
FEELS BOTTOMLESS.

CHERYL MASON

CHERYL MASON

Cheryl Mason is an expert in Corporate & Customer Relations and helps business owners understand and implement best practices in B2B partnerships, lead acquisition, and customer engagement. She is passionate about helping business owners grow with simple CRM solutions that work! Cheryl has spent almost two decades running businesses and crafting customer solutions. She founded The Business Within CRM to help business owners ensure that their communications systems are streamlined and that their customers are profitable.

Website: http://calendly.com/thebusinesswithincrm

FB/IG: @cherylcrmexpert

For my children, you're my purpose. I will always love you for who you are! For my love and best friend, Steven Page, who is the strongest, most loyal, and incredible man. For my parents, who have provided me with a foundation that allowed me to dream big and taught me that giving is the most rewarding return. For my mother-in-law, for her daily support and creative inspiration. For my sister and family, thank you for standing by my side.

CHAPTER 14

AT THE COST OF EVERYTHING

Judge my "at the cost of everything" decisions. Let your raw emotions guide you when you read this chapter. You may feel negatively about my choices that affected my family so harshly, or perhaps you will feel as if this chapter leads you to find the missing piece of "security" you require to finally commit to a dream you have.

I had been disgusted with myself for a really long time. It had been a weird balance of my determination to help people and playing risk with my family's security, my health, and the future of the most important relationships in my life. If you have ever lost your dignity or feel like it is slipping now, join me in finding dignity for yourself again. Either way, I am an entrepreneur who has made choices that affected the lives of those closest to me, and I'm sharing parts of my story so you can use it to protect your family from what my family and I went through.

Use it to build dignity for yourself again and not let the past hold you back from seeing what is possible for your future. Pass my story along to someone you know who may need to hear it so they don't feel alone. And if possible, use it to acquire a new lens of compassion for those rebuilding. Use it to heal yourself. I don't know your story, but if you're an entrepreneur or planning on being one, you will face—at some point in your journey—the "at the cost of everything" decisions. Your decisions that you're ready to make will not only impact your health, your financial security, and your family, but they will also impact your dignity and self-worth, threatening the relationships you hold dearest to your heart. And these will take longer to repair than anything else.

LOOKING BACK

I had just done a standard check on everything and everyone at my multidisciplinary health clinic. Afterward, I was holding my youngest son, sitting in my office breastfeeding him. He was two days shy of a month old, and that made me two days shy of four weeks post-recovery from a C-section. I had returned to the clinic eight days after he was born. If you're an entrepreneur, you understand the dedication wheel we often find ourselves on.

There were two sessions going on and two people exercising in the conditioning area.

Approximately ten minutes into feeding my newborn, I heard the door jingle as someone came in. I knew where the members were in their routine, and I could still hear them. I looked at the time, and the sessions were midway. I adjusted my son so he detached, and I started to burp him as I walked to the door of my office.

I didn't get two feet out the door when the smell of cigarette smoke hit me. I smiled and said, "One moment, please," turned back to my office and placed my son in his bassinet, grabbed the monitor, and stepped outside the door, leaving it slightly open. The man just inside the clinic entrance door looked at me and said, "Are you Cheryl?"

"Yes," I replied.

"Cheryl Mason?" he asked. I couldn't move any nearer to him, as I was so nauseated by his smell. He kept coming closer and closer to me. He then said, "I've been ordered by the court to seize all assets and your clinic."

At that moment, I felt like every part of me had failed. Pure pain and sadness flooded my body, like when the one person you can't live without just vanishes. In shock, I responded, "I have come to an agreement with my landlord and property manager; this must be a mistake."

"Well, the board that owns this property has voted differently."

I was blindsided and felt deeply betrayed.

Still in shock, I proceeded to walk around the clinic with him, reviewing the assets. I clenched the stroller handles—I hated that he was there; I hated that my newborn son was listening to and smelling him; I hated that I had spent every second of my life for the last six months negotiating loan rates, refinancing leases, creating tax break payment plans, saying bye to staff I had loved working with, and tirelessly going through potential buyers/partners of my company just for it to come down to this moment. My mind was running reels of five-second clips of my family, clients, and staff that would be at a loss because of this place closing. Each cell of my body felt like it had been burned numb, but the pain was still there. My heart felt empty.

I was brought back to reality by the awful smell of his cigarette, which led me to the thought that I could never be a bailiff . . . someone who takes the very last possessions and livelihoods of people and their businesses. He then broke the silence by saying, "It's just my job, beautiful, I mean Cheryl, right?"

Now I was mad. Every part of me wanted to scream, "I *need* this place open! There are client appointments today and the rest of the week and the next!" But I didn't scream. I don't know how I found it in me not to lose it. I calmly looked at him and said, "As health providers, we have a responsibility to complete our clients' treatment and care. Can you please speak with whoever is making the decisions right now to provide us time to complete the treatments that are booked?" I gave him an approximate time of need.

After negotiations, we were granted only nine business days. For nine days I went to the clinic, waited to be let in, and served with all I had, just like I had the day it opened. Nine days of contacting clients, members, and contractors and seeing how we could assist in finding them alternatives to support their needs.

This clinic space had been full of bare exterior walls when I leased it. It was a tenant fit-up, and my spouse and father had done the majority of the demolition and put in long hours of work where commercial licensed trades were not required. This was a clinic where I had spent five months as the lead foreman, going in every morning at 5:30 a.m. to meet the trades and supporting them how I could with their work. This was a clinic where from day one my cousin, mom, and friends showed up to lift, clean, and set things up. This was a clinic where the staff did their onboarding and training in the middle of renovations to help keep opening day on schedule. This was a clinic where management spent weeks supporting with setup, design, painting, and cleaning before the grand opening. This clinic had been fully gutted to the exterior walls, and I drew my vision on blueprint paper and watched it come to life. I loved it.

I will never forget how the whole management team modeled full support for their clients and the clinic right to the end. People talk about debt as currency, but when you build something from nothing and have the right people give a chapter of their lives to carry your mission and you can now no longer provide that support to them, the debt feels bottomless.

At what point do you walk away? At what point do you need to detach from the pain to start healing and spend time with your family? I've had so little family life and self-care over the past three years.

I wasn't done. My body was done, and my soul was done, but my desire to be there for people wasn't done, nor was the need to rectify what I could. Even with our bank accounts being emptied and legal action preventing us from coming back to the clinic and threatening to take our home, I was determined to get staff and clients their belongings, as well as assets that could go toward the debt of closing. My family still needed more of me; I couldn't be done.

Prior to the closure, as soon as one financial institute, leaseholder, and lender were notified of my request to renegotiate, they all started firing their highest bid to gain the most legal rights over me. During negotiations, documentation was even delivered to the hospital by someone who pretended to be a family member while I was having my second child. Prior to, during, and post-closure, we were harassed daily by phone calls, and people would show up at our house. They emptied my bank accounts. Even my spouse's account was emptied without any warning because he had co-signed on a loan.

It just became worse once closure was in action. Imagine you're finally feeling independent again after the recommended six-plus weeks of no driving due to C-section recovery. Having little opportunity and not really feeling mentally ready for being anywhere outside your home, you bravely take your three-month-old and four-year-old to the grocery store that is closest to your house. You're walking the aisles exhausted, wishing you had taken the time to make a list, but the objective had been being in public for a distraction. You're singing quietly to the kids because your oldest is now starting to ask for everything he sees and you're trying to meal plan 101 in your head with songs. Then your oldest son goes silent with no movement, looking over your shoulder. You turn around and see a gentleman you have never seen before. You ask your son if he knows him, and he says, "No. He is following us, Muma." After this man follows you for many aisles while you shop, he stops you at the checkout and doesn't hesitate to speak as loudly as he can to serve you court orders for closing early on a lease on equipment. Everyone is staring.

I realized that day that it will be a long time until I have privacy again in my life. I also realized that there will be external factors that will continue to chip away at my dignity and that I am the only one who can rebuild it.

Before closure, I remember being so consumed by my business that people would talk to me about world issues or community events, and it was a foreign language to me. My thoughts were always racing about the next task I needed to do for the clinic. I remember holding my oldest son when he was our only child and being so fearful that I wouldn't remember what it felt like because I had so many decisions to make in a day. Truthfully, I didn't know when my days would end, and they always started before the sun came up. On nights, I was lucky to be home before he fell asleep, and I would get into bed beside him and fall asleep just to have time with him. I'd wake around 1:00 a.m. to do a couple hours of administrative work and sleep for another hour, then I'd be back into the clinic for clients at 6 or 7 a.m.

My kids are my universe, and my business was my world. The day I decided there was no finding a way to reopen and that staying closed provided protection for our future, my world was gone. I was floating in a universe of people who loved me, and I was weightless with no dignity for myself.

ENTREPRENEURSHIP

"I don't have it in me; not one bit of me has the drive to be an entrepreneur." I've heard this belief many times from people throughout my life. I have always loved to work and always looked forward to what I could contribute and solve for people.

Have you ever mistakenly thought someone's life was perfect because they were an optimistic person? I'm not talking about a half-cup-full attitude when the times get tough, but a person who consistently only smiles at the world? A person who looks at everything as the opportunity of a lifetime?

I've never feared sitting at the table in any man- or woman-dominated industry. I've never felt intimidated by any person in a meeting. There were times I admired their knowledge and delivery on a subject, which made me stumble a bit in conversation, but never where I would back down from the opportunity to learn from them. I've always been a more-than-all personality. I could always find my strengths in all the decisions I made; I could tell in some conversations I had that it made some people uncomfortable and perhaps even disgusted sometimes with my optimism.

I was not cocky or overconfident, I just loved serving people and being among interesting minds. I would get nervous and anxious when closing on a big project or when risk was involved, but at the same time, it always fueled me to want to provide more for the people who didn't take these types of steps in life. As a business owner, I was all heart.

Some say it clouded my judgment on some decisions, but if I would have followed only logic, my clinic would have never opened, nor would I have known how to pivot through the first couple of months we were open in my first year.

I'm telling you all of this about my personality before the bankruptcy because you need to know I had never dealt with nor was aware of how to deal with anxiety, depression, lack of self-worth, and debilitating stress levels until my business started not surviving.

PROTECTION

We often think of "protection" as something that is a physical act when it comes to our families or ourselves. To protect the human body, we prepare healthy food and participate in physical activity. We bathe for good hygiene, we learn life skills, and we dive to catch our children when they're about to face danger. As a business owner, you also have to protect your family by ensuring you have the correct knowledge needed to keep your personal assets safe.

Although people with no assets under their name walk away with very little financial burden post-bankruptcy, that was not my case. While the following is not to be taken as formal legal advice, I do encourage reviewing your operations and personal liability before launching, as well as often throughout your business life cycle, with a lawyer, accountant, and a Licensed Insolvency Trustee. This is something I wish I would have done annually in more detail to align with the growing demands of my business.

NAVIGATING BANKRUPTCY WITH DIGNITY

As entrepreneurs, we may have been self-taught or exposed to the formal learning of financial risk, but it was most likely only financial management. Even when you're a financially responsible person, someone who saves 50 percent of their paycheck, has all the right savings accounts, and never spends past a comfort level on their credit card, the threshold of entrepreneurial risk has never been taught.

You may have been taught that incorporating your business is protection for yourself. It is not protection for your personal assets. We might have told ourselves that the success of our businesses will directly result in how we provide for our families. Success doesn't take care of our families, we do. We might think our boundaries are clearly set and that they will keep our loved ones close to us. But then when you're finally removed, you see that the majority who own a business battle through these trenches, nicking their arms and legs on each sharp decision made along the way, while dragging their loved ones through their emotional "at the cost of everything" roller coaster of decisions. We become distant instead of being present in the moments that matter, and the deep connections we think we have with loved ones begin thinning. Who are the fortunate few who sustain their dignity with their family by their side after the trenches are filled and paved over?

Bankruptcy should never be your strategy or exit plan when going into ownership of a business. Bankruptcy is protection when everything else has been exhausted.

As a business owner, the responsibility is yours to be proactive so that if you need to one day use this protection to sustain your family and personal well-being, you can. My wish is that you're prepared so that my story never happens to you. If you don't have yourself protected and you're nearing the decision of closure, find comfort knowing that you're not alone. Hear this:

You won't feel like yourself for a very long time. That's okay. You will need to pull back and detach yourself from any label you have ever worn. That's okay. You won't ever be the same person you were before. That's okay. You may live in fear that the strain on your family will grow again. That's the most painful part, but that's okay too. All of this will lead you to a new chapter in your life. And that's okay.

A NEW CHAPTER IN MY LIFE

What I have learned while healing throughout these last couple years is that your perception of yourself is the most expensive thing you will ever carry with you, not any transaction of debt.

To prepare for our new chapter in life, we tend to reevaluate our values and priorities. We make lists of goals and steps to achieve the lifestyle we want. If your life is already driven by lists, alarms, and cramming as much as possible into a day as mine was, this can sometimes add to the overwhelming chaos when healing. What I found supported my process of recovery and I still use daily is this: What actions in my life today will free up tomorrow? Because we never know what will be of greater importance tomorrow or who in our life will need us. Freeing up tomorrow is empowering because it provides you with a choice.

Reflecting back, we had a five-star collaborative multidisciplinary health clinic with raving positive results from clients. What we didn't have was retention processes, an optimized CRM system, referral programs, and growing funnels to bring in new leads. I was approached by a couple of companies to be a consultant on Customer and Corporate Relations after my clinic closure. I was asked to design new innovative ways to keep their customers engaged, forecast their customer lifecycles, find new streams of revenue, and maintain their strongest streams of revenue, all while they pivoted through COVID-19. One contract led to another, and I'm now known as the "CRM Expert." Today, I'm dedicated to entrepreneurs who need someone focused on bringing in quality leads, retention, and customer engagement strategies that are innovative to their industry as well as profitable.

There will always be people who know why your business ended. You might even feel strongly about why mine closed. The simple truth is that some businesses end because a new chapter in life is starting. People in business don't sit with enough past business owners to find out why their business failed, ended, closed, or why they won't try again. We tend to only want to learn from the successful ones.

Whether this is your first business or your tenth, you don't need permission to let go of your past labels, either created by you or by others, even if you can still see these labels like huge billboard signs as you move through your life or in the odd time when you look in the mirror.

I've started over as a business owner, but the experience and knowledge I have are richer than ever before. I'm truly addicted to how businesses grow, thanks to my story. I'm in a totally different career now, working on companies within multiple industries, both product- and service-based, and I'm loving it! It's vastly different from what I had daydreamed about for the first 30+ years of my life. And that's okay. The businesses I'm consulting for right now and the future companies where I will make positive growth all hold a puzzle piece of "My Why" I'm an entrepreneur. "My Purpose" in life will always be my children.

My story, which I've partly shared with you in this chapter, is an opportunity for you to pin my support on your shoulder, stand taller, and know that your dignity and survival are within you! Join me in honoring the differences within your everyday life between your "why" and your "purpose." The clearer these two elements of your life become, the more your life will be revealed.

Use your "why" and "purpose" to build dignity for yourself when you need a refill. Revisit internally often to see if your past is holding you back from being a part of what is possible for your future. Take comfort in the fact that success comes in many different definitions. Mostly, you must define these yourself. Invest in your self-worth: it is your gateway so you can confidently embrace challenges. Do what you can to free up your tomorrow, for tomorrow might be harder, bring new opportunities, or be the gift that it is as itself. At the cost of any decision in the end, you need to tell yourself, "That's okay" and heal.

The journey of "mamapreneurship" is not an easy one. It can be full of dramatic highs and crushing lows. It can be extremely fulfilling at times, but also uncomfortable and heart-wrenching at other times. Most of all, being a mom entrepreneur can be incredibly lonely.

When I launched my first business, I had two babies, a full-time job, a side hustle, and a dream. I had no clue what I was doing or how I would make it work. But guess what? I figured it out.

WHAT I'VE LEARNED ALONG THE WAY

First off, I made the decision to move through the discomfort and embrace the hard stuff. My journey wasn't perfect. I made mistakes . . . a LOT of them! But I didn't let them paralyze me. Instead, I chose to keep getting up each morning and taking action. Sometimes those actions were big and scary, but often they were small and seemingly insignificant. Some days I felt like I was getting further ahead, and other days the progress was not so obvious. But by choosing "growth" over "comfort," I gradually became a better entrepreneur and, I believe, a better person.

Next, I realized that if I was to become a successful coach that I would need to stop fretting over what everyone else thought. The reality was that I didn't know a lot of people who were doing what I had chosen to do. Most of my friends had day jobs, and while they were all very dear, supportive people, they couldn't possibly understand the struggles that entrepreneurship presents. I felt awkward posting social media videos of myself talking about my coaching work because I worried about what people would think of me. But I had to stop caring about their potential judgment as I started showing up more online and sharing my opinions on social media. I had to stop worrying about being liked. Instead, I had to show the world the real me!

And finally, I made the brilliant decision that I was not going to go it alone. I hope you take this message that has permeated almost every chapter within these pages:

We were not meant to do it all alone!

As mothers, as leaders . . . heck, as humans! We are all stronger together. But somehow many of us have been conditioned along the way that we must struggle in silence when times get hard. We've been programmed to think that asking for help is a sign of weakness. We continue to act out societal expectations, soldiering on with smiles on our faces as "good girls" do. We assume we have to know everything and solve everything on our own. After all, isn't that what our mothers taught us?

The truth is that I've grown more in the last decade *because* I asked for help, not in spite of it. I'm a better version of myself because I rely on the strength of others to help me accomplish my dreams.

WHAT MY WOMEN HAVE TAUGHT ME

Along my journey, there's a lot that I've learned about running a business from coaches, mentors, and peers. But there's also a lot that I've learned from my clients. In fact, I've had the immense pleasure of getting to coach and guide all the authors in this book at some point in their journey, and here's what they have taught me:

IMPOSTOR SYNDROME IS UNIVERSAL

There has not been a single woman that I have coached in the last eight years that has not experienced some form of impostor syndrome. Even the most confident of business leaders will experience a feeling of "not good enough" at some point in their journey. This feeling, while incredibly debilitating, is also very normal. The secret is that you can't let it stop you. Feel the doubts and be willing to work through them so you can put them behind you.

There is no magic cure for impostor syndrome except to keep moving forward. Show up. Share your infinite wisdom. Serve your people from the heart. Don't make it about you, make it about them. Keep their needs and pain points in mind as you build your business. They're the ones who will see you through the difficult times, and they already know you are enough!

WE ARE FURTHER THAN WE THINK WE ARE

As I always say to my clients, you don't have to be miles ahead of your clients—a little ahead is okay. You may think you're "not an expert," as I hear so often in my coaching work, but you *are* an expert to *someone*!

Don't believe me? Take a moment to share something on your social media in the next few days, something you're certain of or feel strongly about. Post it with confidence and from the heart and watch what happens. When you have the courage to step up, people will respond. When you have the courage to be a leader, even before you feel ready, people will start to see you that way.

My clients are creating progress every day, and it's such a joy to watch them build success over time. They remind me that we are all better than we think.

LEADERS COME IN ALL SHAPES AND SIZES

You don't have to have a PhD or an MBA to be a leader. Trust me, I'm living proof of this! The amazing authors in this book are all leaders in their own right. Some are leading as educators, helping their clients learn new skills. Some are community leaders, bringing people together over common goals. Others are leading teams of people, helping others gain valuable work experience and grow their careers. And some, like myself, are leading movements, helping change the world with their groundbreaking work.

But there's one thing they all have in common: none of them felt like leaders when they were first starting out. And that's because confidence comes from having the courage to do the things that most people won't.

WE ALL DESERVE SUPPORT

There is not a single woman who contributed to this book who hasn't invested in support. These women are confident enough in themselves to know what they don't know. Thus, they invest in virtual assistants, tech support, customer service, graphic designers, coaches, and consultants to help them get further, faster. And while they could do a lot of these tasks on their own, these women are wise enough to recognize the power of asking for (and paying for) great help!

By investing in other female entrepreneurs and small businesses, they are supporting another woman and her family, they are contributing to the growth of the economy, and they are helping spread more wealth, joy, and abundance. These women are paying it forward every day!

WHAT WILL YOU TAKE WITH YOU?

I curated this book with the aim of helping mom entrepreneurs feel more supported in the choices they make. I brought together the women whose stories educate and inspire. My goal is that you, the reader, have more than a dozen examples of women just like you who are living their dreams while overcoming the obstacles that life throws at them.

If they can do it, so can you!

As you journey forth, I hope that you'll take with you a sense of what is possible. I hope you leave with a sense of deep knowing that you can make a difference in this world, regardless of your age, experience, or background. I hope you have the courage to take that first step, no matter how scary it may feel. But most of all, I hope you move forward with an ever-present trust in yourself.

You have everything inside you to be the mother, business owner, and leader that you dream of being. Your setbacks, your experiences, are not hindrances to your success but catalysts. Let your wounds propel you forward. Use your life experiences to fuel you and arm you with the tools to transform into the woman you want to become.

COLLECTIVE ACKNOWLEDGMENTS

This collection of essays has been a true labor of love, and we, the authors, would be remiss if we didn't take a few moments to appreciate all the people in our lives that helped us get here.

TO OUR FAMILIES

You are the ones who raised us; you are the ones who shaped us. You made us who we are today. For good or bad, we are where we are today because of you. Your support, guidance, and encouragement have been invaluable, and we appreciate all you have done to help us create the lives we have.

TO OUR FRIENDS AND PEERS

Everyone needs a shoulder to lean on, and this group all relies on the support of friends and peers to help lift us higher when times are tough and to share in the wins. The road of entrepreneurship is not an easy one, so we wish to thank all our dear friends who have shared in the journey with us. Thank you for always being there.

TO OUR TEAMS

Each and every badass businesswoman needs a team of badass women (and men) behind them, and this group is no exception. Everyone who contributed to this book has relied on the help of other small business owners to help get them where they are today. We would not be where we are without the support of these team members.

TO OUR CLIENTS

Small business owners rely on the support of customers to achieve their goals. This group is proud to say we have some of the best customers anyone could ask for. In fact, we are all proud to have true Dream Clients in our world who support us, promote us, buy from us, and share our offerings with their friends. Customers are the lifeblood of any business, so we thank you for supporting our dreams.

TO OUR MENTORS AND COACHES

The women in this book have all invested in personal and professional growth, often working with coaches and mentors, sometimes more than one at a time! It is said that success leaves clues, and we agree. We are grateful for the guidance and support of those who have gone before us and shared their knowledge willingly and generously so that we, too, may experience success and abundance. It takes a very special person to be a mentor, and we thank them for stepping up to the challenge.

TO OUR PUBLISHING TEAM

Thank you for all the hard work and love you have poured into this project. We know that managing different personalities on a project like this is not easy (especially when on a tight timeline), so we thank you from the bottom of our hearts for making this book the very best it could be.

TO OUR COAUTHORS

We are grateful for the camaraderie of our fellow authors on this project. The women in this book are strong, smart, and fierce but also incredibly kind and giving. We appreciate the support you have lent along the way, as it has helped us have the courage to step up and be vulnerable. Becoming a published author is not for the faint of heart, and we are grateful to have had some amazing women to share in the journey.

TO OUR FAITH

Many of our authors identify as religious or spiritual. We are grateful for the higher powers that have allowed for our gifts to emerge so that this book can touch the lives of others.

TO OUR PARTNERS

This group is blessed to have the support of many loving partners. It is not easy to share a life with an entrepreneur, especially while raising children, and our partners work hard so that we can live our dreams.

TO OUR CHILDREN

We wrote this book for you so that you can learn about the path we took to get here. We want you to know how much we love you. We want to inspire you to follow your own dreams and become great leaders. The world needs more of what you have to give. You are our "why," and we are forever grateful for all the lessons you have taught us.

WHAT'S NEXT?

Well, friend,

I'm hopeful this book has inspired you to start or grow your mamapreneur business, despite any challenges life may throw at you. If you are ready to take that next step, here are three ways we can continue the journey:

MY COMMUNITY!

Are you a mom with a business or plans to start one? Then we want to welcome you into my incredible community of mom bosses . . . Mamas & Co. Simply visit **www.mamasandco.com** to find out more!

MY PODCAST!

Every week I share my best nugget of wisdom and inspiration on my podcast, *The Business of Thinking Big*. You can find it on iTunes, Spotify, the Apple Podcast App, and anywhere you listen to podcasts, or visit my website: **www. liannekim.com/blog**

MY BOOK!

If you enjoyed this book, then you'll also likely enjoy my first and best-selling book, *Building a Joyful Business*, where I give you step-by-step guidance on how to build a business and life you love. You can pick up a copy at liannekim. com/book

Thanks, and I hope to connect again soon!

Lianne

Mamas
& CO.

@mamasandco

@mamasandco

@mamasandco

YGTMedia Co. is a blended boutique publishing house for mission-driven humans. We help seasoned and emerging authors "birth their brain babies" through a supportive and collaborative approach. Specializing in narrative nonfiction and adult and children's empowerment books, we believe that words can change the world, and we intend to do so one book at a time.

ygtmedia.co/publishing

@ygtmedia.company

@ygtmedia.co